Ben Stacy Jerrik (Ed.)

Status Bar

Ben Stacy Jerrik (Ed.)

Status Bar

Window (computing), Graphical user interface, Web browser

Part Press

Imprint

Publisher:
Part Press is a trademark of
International Book Market Service Ltd., 17 Rue Meldrum, Beau Bassin, 1713-01 Mauritius
Email: info@bookmarketservice.com
Website: www.bookmarketservice.com

Published in 2012

Printed in: U.S.A., U.K., Germany. This book was not produced in Mauritius.

ISBN: 978-613-6-46284-4

Contents

Articles

References

Status_bar

```
----:---F1  *scratch*         (Lisp Interaction)--L1--All-------------------
```

An example of a status bar in Emacs

A **status bar**, similar to a **status line**, is an information area typically found at the bottom of windows in a graphical user interface.[1] A status bar is sometimes divided into sections, each of which shows different information. Its job is primarily to display information about the current state of its window, although some status bars have extra functionality. For example, many web browsers have clickable sections that pop up a display of security or privacy information.

A status bar can also be text-based, primarily in console-based applications, in which case it is usually the last row in an 80x25 text mode configuration, leaving the top 24 rows for application data. Usually, the status bar, typically called a *status line* in this context, displays the current state of the application, plus helpful keyboard shortcuts, such as in the 'vi' text editor of UNIX (from the 1970s) or newer Linux systems.[2]

Status lines have been used for more than 30 years[2] to display advisory messages in a predefined area, rather than as pop-up messages in center screen which can block the view of related information behind the pop-up messages. Although pop-up windows could be used to focus attention, status lines with contrasting hightlighting or colors can also be used to focus attention, without blocking the view.

Sometimes, a video game places the player's vital information (such as hit points, lives, and score) on a similar strip across the bottom or top of the screen; this is also referred to as a status bar.

A status bar can be implemented during software development as a component (widget) in a window in a graphical user interface. [1]

Examples

- The status bar of a file manager often shows the count of items in the current directory, their total size, or the size of the currently selected item.
- The status bar of a web browser will sit relatively dormant when the user is viewing on a page, then light up with a flourish of activity when the user clicks a link.
- The status bar of a graphics editor will show information about the current image, such as its dimensions, colour space, or resolution.
- In a word processor, the status bar often shows cursor position, the number of pages in the document, and the state of the caps lock, num lock, and scroll lock keys. Additionally, many word processors assign the insert key a behaviour similar to that of these three, to allow toggling the insertion mode – the state of that is also displayed in the status bar.
- Text adventures often had a status line that displayed information such as the players location, game time, and score. Infocom's customer newsletter was named *The Status Line*
- In a spreadsheet, the status bar shows similar information to word processors, but includes the ability to highlight cells and show the average, sum, maximum value, and so forth.

Status bars allow split-window interface

Status bars, and status lines before them, have been used for years[2] to display advisory messages in a predefined area, rather than as pop-up messages in center screen which can block the view of related information behind the pop-up messages. The use of status bars (or status lines) involves both advantages and disadvantages:

Advantages of status bars:

- status bars allow viewing messages while viewing the total screen;
- status bars allow typing information while viewing status data;
- status bars allow other menu options while viewing status data;
- status bars can continually show status during operation.

Disadvantages of status bars:

- status bars might restrict information to a one-line display (although a variable multi-line status bar/region could be used);
- status bars typically cannot pop to the surface for critical messages.

Although pop-up windows could be used to focus attention, status lines with contrasting hightlighting or colors can also be used to focus attention, without blocking the view.

See also

- Other window bars: menu bar, toolbar, address bar.

Notes

[1] "GTK+ and Glade3 GUI Programming Tutorial - Part 1", Micah Carrick, December 2007, webpage: GUI-tutorial-status-bar (http://www.micahcarrick.com/12-24-2007/gtk-glade-tutorial-part-1.html).

[2] "How to Use the vi Editor*", Univ. of Washington, Simon Fraser University, 1991, webpage: WEdu-Unix-vi (http://www.washington.edu/computing/unix/vi.html).

Window_(computing)

In computing, a **window** is a visual area containing some kind of user interface. It usually has a rectangular shape[1] that can overlap with the area of other windows. It displays the **output** of and may allow **input** to one or more processes.

Windows are primarily associated with graphical displays, where they can be manipulated with a pointer.

A graphical user interface (GUI) using windows as one of its main "metaphors" is called a windowing system.

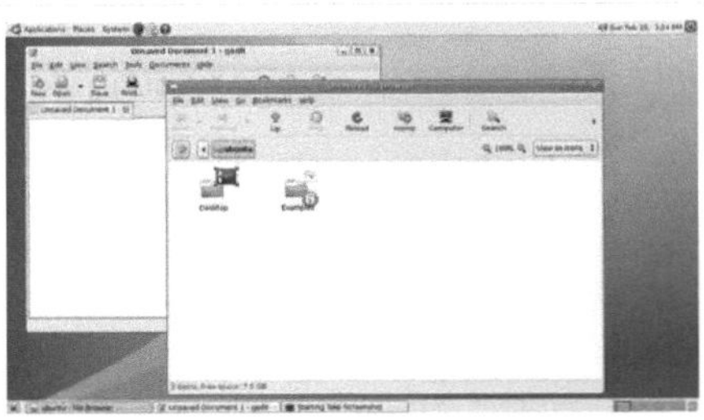

An example of some windows in a graphical user interface - GNOME. Two application windows are displayed. Note that one partly overlaps the other.

Properties

Windows are two dimensional objects arranged on a plane called the desktop. In a modern full-featured windowing system they can be resized, moved, hidden, restored or closed.

Windows usually include other graphical objects, possibly including a menu-bar, toolbars, controls, icons and often a working area. In the working area, the document, image, folder contents or other main object is displayed. Around the working area, within the bounding window, there may be other smaller window areas, sometimes called panes or panels, showing relevant information or options. The working area of a single document interface holds only one main object. "Child windows" in multiple document interfaces, and tabs for example in many web browsers, can make several similar documents or main objects available within a single main application window.

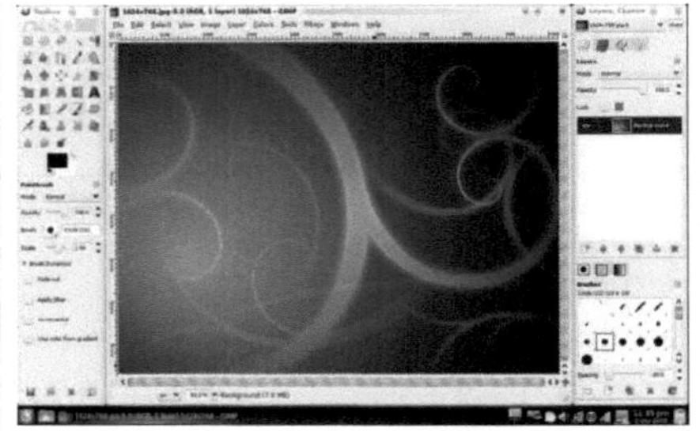

The GIMP, a multi-window image manipulation program

Some windows in Mac OS X have a feature called a drawer, which is a pane that slides out the side of the window and to show extra options without cluttering the main window space.

History

The idea was developed at the Stanford Research Institute (led by Douglas Engelbart).[2] Their earliest systems supported multiple windows, but there was no obvious way to indicate boundaries between them (such as window borders, title bars, etc.).[3]

Research continued at Xerox Corporation's Palo Alto Research Center / PARC (led by Alan Kay). They used overlapping windows.[4]

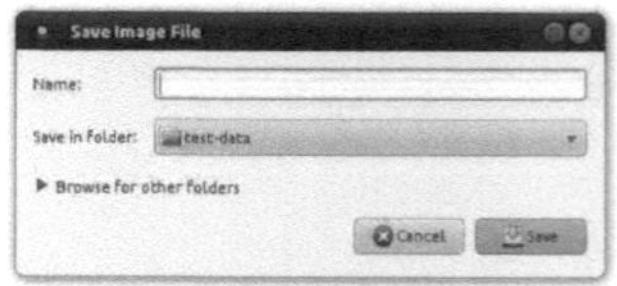

A "Save as..." file dialog from GTK+

During the 1980s the term "WIMP", which stands for window, icon, menu, pointer, was coined at PARC.

Apple had worked with PARC briefly at that time. Apple developed an interface based on PARC's interface. It was first used on Apple's Lisa and later Macintosh computers.[1] Microsoft was developing office applications for the "Mac" at that time. Some speculate that this gave them access to Apple's OS before it was released and thus influenced the design of the windowing system in what would eventually be called Windows.[5]

Window managers

The part of a windowing system which manages window operations is called a *window manager*.[6]

Examples of some current windowing systems:

- DEC Windows (for VMS)
- X Window System (for GNU & Unix-like systems)
- Microsoft Windows
- Sun's OpenWindows

See also

- Window manager
- Graphical user interface
- Human interface guidelines
- WIMP (computing)

References

[1] Reimer, Jeremy (2005). "A History of the GUI (Part 3)" (http://arstechnica.com/old/content/2005/05/gui.ars/3). Ars Technica. . Retrieved 2009-09-14.

[2] Reimer, Jeremy (2005). "A History of the GUI (Part 1)" (http://arstechnica.com/old/content/2005/05/gui.ars). Ars Technica. . Retrieved 2009-09-14.

[3] Reimer, Jeremy (2005). "A History of the GUI (Part 2)" (http://arstechnica.com/old/content/2005/05/gui.ars/2). Ars Technica. . Retrieved 2009-09-14.

[4] "Milestones: 1975 - Graphical User Interface (GUI)" (http://www.parc.com/about/milestones.html). Palo Alto Research Center Incorporated. . Retrieved 2009-09-14.

[5] Reimer, Jeremy (2005). "A History of the GUI (Part 5)" (http://arstechnica.com/old/content/2005/05/gui.ars/5). Ars Technica. . Retrieved 2009-09-14.

[6] Barger, Jorn (2002). "Linux desktops (GUIs, widgets, window managers, etc)" (http://www.robotwisdom.com/linux/desktops.html). . Retrieved 2009-09-14.

Graphical_user_interface

In computing, a **graphical user interface** (**GUI**, commonly pronounced *gooey*[1]) is a type of user interface that allows users to interact with electronic devices using images rather than text commands. *GUI*s can be used in computers, hand-held devices such as MP3 players, portable media players or gaming devices, household appliances and office equipment. A *GUI* represents the information and actions available to a user through graphical icons and visual indicators such as secondary notation, as opposed to text-based interfaces, typed command labels or text navigation. The actions are usually performed through direct manipulation of the graphical elements.[2]

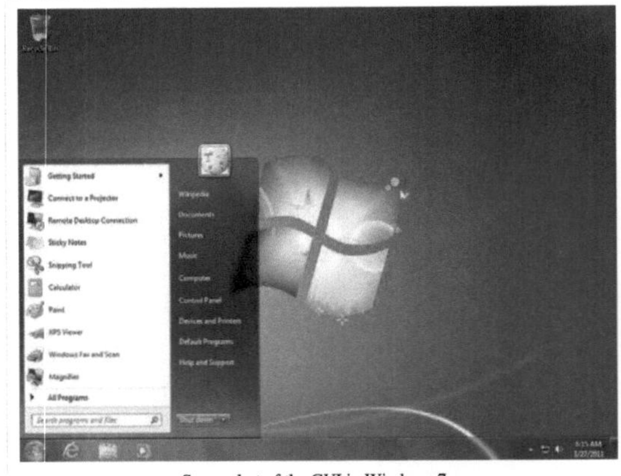

Screenshot of the GUI in Windows 7 .

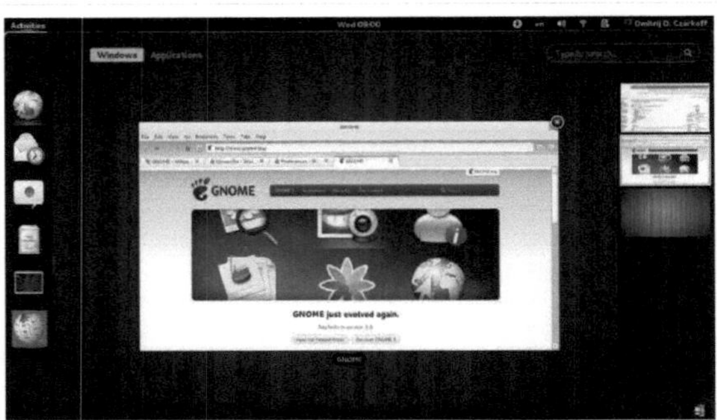

A screenshot of the GNOME Shell GUI.

The term *GUI* is restricted to the scope of two-dimensional display screens with display resolutions able to describe generic information, in the tradition of the computer science research at the PARC (Palo Alto Research Center). The term *GUI* is rarely applied to other high-resolution types of interfaces that are non-generic, such as video games (where HUD[3] is preferred), or not restricted to flat screens, like volumetric displays.[4]

The Xerox Alto was the first to use a graphical user interface.

History

Precursors

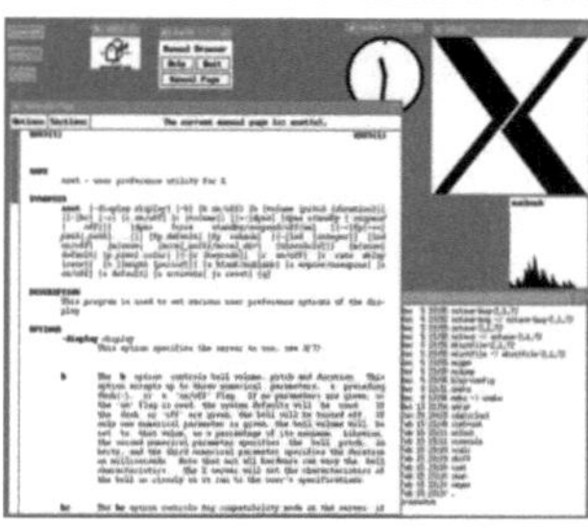

An early-1990s style Unix desktop running the X Window System graphical user interface

A precursor to GUIs was invented by researchers at the Stanford Research Institute, led by Douglas Engelbart. They developed the use of text-based hyperlinks manipulated with a mouse for the On-Line System. The concept of hyperlinks was further refined and extended to graphics by researchers at Xerox PARC, specifically Alan Kay, who went beyond text-based hyperlinks and used a GUI as the primary interface for the Xerox Alto computer. Most modern general-purpose GUIs are derived from this system.

Ivan Sutherland developed a pointer-based system called the Sketchpad in 1963. It used a light-pen to guide the creation and manipulation of objects in engineering drawings.

PARC user interface

The PARC user interface consisted of graphical elements such as windows, menus, radio buttons, check boxes and icons. The PARC user interface employs a pointing device in addition to a keyboard. These aspects can be emphasized by using the alternative acronym WIMP, which stands for *windows*, *icons*, *menus* and *pointing device*.

Evolution

Following PARC the first GUI-centric computer operating model was the Xerox 8010 Star Information System in 1981,[5] followed by the Apple Lisa (which presented the concept of menu bar as well as window controls) in 1983, the Apple Macintosh 128K in 1984, and the Atari ST and Commodore Amiga in 1985.

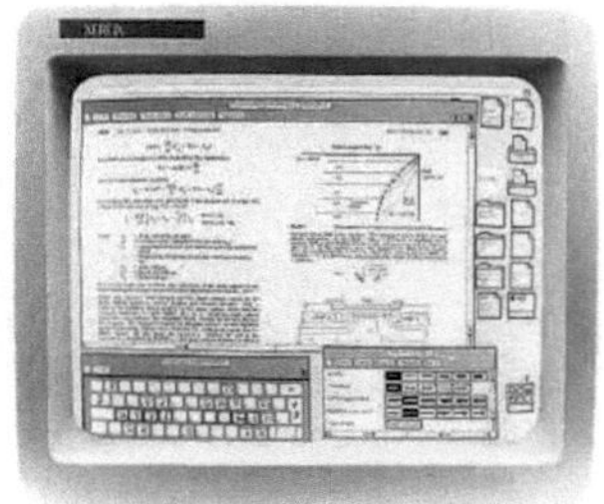

The Xerox Star Workstation introduced the first commercial GUI operating system as shown above.

The early GUI commands, until the advent of the IBM's Common User Access, [6] used different command sequences for different programs. A command like the F3 function key activated help in WordPerfect, but exited an IBM program. The menus were accessed by different keys (control in WordStar, Alt or F10 in Microsoft programs, "/" in Lotus 1-2-3, F9 in Norton Commander to name a few common ones).

To this end, the early software came with keyboard overlays. These are plastic or paper masks which sit over the empty space between the keys, providing the user with the named application's use of various keys. Even today, different keystrokes exist with radically different calls. For example, the Control-Alt-Delete interface is intercepted in Windows to invoke a task menu. In Unix PC-systems, this usually invokes an automatic shutdown.

The GUIs familiar to most people today are Microsoft Windows, Mac OS X, and X Window System interfaces for desktop and laptop computers, and Symbian, BlackBerry OS, Android and Apple's iOS for handheld ("smartphone") devices.

Apple, IBM and Microsoft used many of Xerox's ideas to develop products, and IBM's Common User Access specifications formed the basis of the user interface found in Microsoft Windows, IBM OS/2 Presentation Manager, and the Unix Motif toolkit and window manager. These ideas evolved to create the interface found in current versions of Microsoft Windows, as well as in Mac OS X and various desktop environments for Unix-like operating systems, such as Linux. Thus most current GUIs have largely common idioms.

Components

Further information: WIMP (computing), Window manager, and Desktop environment

A GUI uses a combination of technologies and devices to provide a platform that the user can interact with, for the tasks of gathering and producing information.

A series of elements conforming a visual language have evolved to represent information stored in computers. This makes it easier for people with few computer skills to work with and use computer software. The most common combination of such elements in GUIs is the WIMP ("window, icon, menu, pointing device") paradigm, especially in personal computers.

The WIMP style of interaction uses a physical input device to control the position of a pointer and presents information organized in windows and represented with icons. Available commands are compiled together in menus, and actions are performed making gestures with the pointing device. A window manager facilitates the interactions between windows, applications, and the windowing system. The windowing system handles hardware devices such as pointing devices and graphics hardware, as well as the positioning of the pointer.

In personal computers all these elements are modeled through a desktop metaphor, to produce a simulation called a desktop environment in which the display represents a desktop, upon which documents and folders of documents can be placed. Window managers and other software combine to simulate the desktop environment with varying degrees of realism.

Post-WIMP interfaces

Smaller mobile devices such as PDAs and smartphones typically use the WIMP elements with different unifying metaphors, due to constraints in space and available input devices. Applications for which WIMP is not well suited may use newer interaction techniques, collectively named as post-WIMP user interfaces.[7]

As of 2011, some touch-screen-based operating systems such as Apple's iOS (iPhone) and Android use the class of GUIs named post-WIMP. These support styles of interaction using more than one finger in contact with a display, which allows actions such as pinching and rotating, which are unsupported by one pointer and mouse.[8]

Post-WIMP includes 3D compositing window managers such as Compiz, Desktop Window Manager, and LG3D. Some post-WIMP interfaces may be better suited for applications which model immersive 3D environments, such as Google Earth.[9]

User interface and interaction design

Designing the visual composition and temporal behavior of GUI is an important part of software application programming in the area of human-computer interaction. Its goal is to enhance the efficiency and ease of use for the underlying logical design of a stored program, a design discipline known as usability. Methods of user-centered design are used to ensure that the visual language introduced in the design is well tailored to the tasks.

The visible graphical interface features of an application are sometimes referred to as "chrome".[10] [11] Typically, the user interacts with information by manipulating visual widgets that allow for interactions appropriate to the kind of data they hold. The widgets of a well-designed interface are selected to support the actions necessary to achieve the goals of the user. A model-view-controller allows for a flexible structure in which the interface is independent from and indirectly linked to application functionality, so the GUI can be easily customized. This allows the user to select or design a different *skin* at will, and eases the designer's work to change the interface as the user needs evolve. Good user interface design relates to the user, not the system architecture.

Large widgets, such as windows, usually provide a frame or container for the main presentation content such as a web page, email message or drawing. Smaller ones usually act as a user-input tool.

A GUI may be designed for the requirements of a vertical market as application-specific graphical user interfaces. Examples of application-specific GUIs are:

- Automated teller machines (ATM)
- Point-Of-Sale touchscreens at restaurants [12]
- Self-service checkouts used in a retail store
- Airline self-ticketing and check-in
- Information kiosks in a public space, like a train station or a museum
- Monitors or control screens in an embedded industrial application which employ a real time operating system (RTOS).

The latest cell phones and handheld game systems also employ application specific touchscreen GUIs. Newer automobiles use GUIs in their navigation systems and touch screen multimedia centers.

Comparison to other interfaces

Command-line interfaces

Modern CLI

GUIs were introduced in reaction to the perceived steep learning curve of command-line interfaces (CLI),[13] [14] [14] which require commands to be typed on the keyboard. Since the commands available in command line interfaces can be numerous, complicated operations can be completed using a short sequence of words and symbols. This allows for greater efficiency and productivity once many commands are learned,[13] [14] [14] but reaching this level takes some time because the command words are not easily discoverable and not mnemonic. WIMPs ("window, icon, menu, pointing device"), on the other hand, present the user with numerous widgets that represent and can trigger some of the system's available commands.

On the other hand, GUIs can be made quite hard by burying dialogs deep in the system, or moving dialogs from place to place. Also, dialog boxes are considerably harder for the user to script.

WIMPs extensively use modes as the meaning of all keys and clicks on specific positions on the screen are redefined all the time. Command line interfaces use modes only in limited forms, such as the current directory and environment variables.

Most modern operating systems provide both a GUI and some level of a CLI, although the GUIs usually receive more attention. The GUI is usually WIMP-based, although occasionally other metaphors surface, such as those used in Microsoft Bob, 3dwm or File System Visualizer (FSV).

Applications may also provide both interfaces, and when they do the GUI is usually a WIMP wrapper around the command-line version. This is especially common with applications designed for Unix-like operating systems. The latter used to be implemented first because it allowed the developers to focus exclusively on their product's functionality without bothering about interface details such as designing icons and placing buttons. Designing programs this way also allows users to run the program non-interactively, such as in a shell script.

Three-dimensional user interfaces

For typical computer displays, *three-dimensional* is a misnomer—their displays are two-dimensional. Semantically, however, most graphical user interfaces use three dimensions - in addition to height and width, they offer a third dimension of layering or stacking screen elements over one another. This may be represented visually on screen through an illusionary transparent effect, which offers the advantage that information in background windows may still be read, if not interacted with. Or the environment may simply hide the background information, possibly making the distinction apparent by drawing a drop shadow effect over it.

Some environments use the methods of 3D graphics to project virtual three dimensional user interface objects onto the screen. As the processing power of computer graphics hardware increases, this becomes less of an obstacle to a smooth user experience.

Three-dimensional graphics are currently mostly used in computer games, art and computer-aided design (CAD). A three-dimensional computing environment could also be useful in other scenarios, like molecular graphics and aircraft design.

Several attempts have been made to create a multi-user three-dimensional environment, including the Croquet Project and Sun's Project Looking Glass.

Technologies

The use of three-dimensional graphics has become increasingly common in mainstream operating systems, from creating attractive interfaces—eye candy— to functional purposes only possible using three dimensions. For example, user switching is represented by rotating a cube whose faces are each user's workspace, and window management is represented via a Rolodex-style flipping mechanism in Windows Vista (see Windows Flip 3D). In both cases, the operating system transforms windows on-the-fly while continuing to update the content of those windows.

Interfaces for the X Window System have also implemented advanced three-dimensional user interfaces through compositing window managers such as Beryl, Compiz and KWin using the AIGLX or XGL architectures, allowing for the usage of OpenGL to animate the user's interactions with the desktop.

Another branch in the three-dimensional desktop environment is the three-dimensional GUIs that take the desktop metaphor a step further, like the BumpTop, where a user can manipulate documents and windows as if they were "real world" documents, with realistic movement and physics.

The Zooming User Interface (ZUI) is a related technology that promises to deliver the representation benefits of 3D environments without their usability drawbacks of orientation problems and hidden objects. It is a logical advancement on the GUI, blending some three-dimensional movement with two-dimensional or "2.5D" vector objects. In 2006, Hillcrest Labs introduced the first zooming user interface for television.[15]

In science fiction

Three-dimensional GUIs appeared in science fiction literature and movies before they were technically feasible or in common use. For example, the 1993 American film *Jurassic Park* features Silicon Graphics' three-dimensional file manager File System Navigator, a real-life file manager for Unix operating systems. In prose fiction, three-dimensional user interfaces have been displayed as immersible environments like William Gibson's Cyberspace or Neal Stephenson's Metaverse.

See also

- Apple v. Microsoft
- Computer icon
- Distinguishable interfaces
- Ergonomics
- General graphics interface
- Look and feel
- Natural user interface (NUI)
- Ncurses
- Object-oriented user interface
- Organic User Interface
- Rich Internet applications
- Skin
- Text entry interface
- Text user interface (TUI)
- User interface engineering
- Vector-Based GUI
- Worrell

References

[1] "Definition of GUI at Dictionary.com" (http://dictionary.reference.com/browse/GUI). . Retrieved January 2010.

[2] "window manager Definition" (http://www.pcmag.com/encyclopedia_term/0,2542,t=window+manager&i=54598,00.asp). *PC Magazine*. Ziff Davis Publishing Holdings Inc.. . Retrieved 12 November 2008.

[3] Greg Wilson (2006). "Off With Their HUDs!: Rethinking the Heads-Up Display in Console Game Design" (http://www.gamasutra.com/features/20060203/wilson_01.shtml). *Gamasutra*. . Retrieved February 14, 2006.

[4] "GUI definition" (http://www.linfo.org/gui.html). *Linux Information Project*. October 1, 2004. . Retrieved 12 November 2008.

[5] The first GUIs (http://www.catb.org/~esr/writings/taouu/html/ch02s05.html)

[6] IBM, Systems Application Architecture: Common User Access: Basic Interface Design Guide, Document SC26-4583-00 (http://publibz.boulder.ibm.com/cgi-bin/bookmgr/BOOKS/F29BDG00/3.7?DT=19921204095534), 1992.

[7] IEEE.org. (http://ieeexplore.ieee.org/Xplore/login.jsp?url=/iel5/38/17635/00814559.pdf?isnumber=17635&prod=JNL&arnumber=814559&arSt=50&ared=51&arAuthor=van+Dam,+A)

[8] Tufts.edu (http://www.cs.tufts.edu/~jacob/papers/chi08.pdf)

[9] Arcada.fi (http://people.arcada.fi/~johnny/postwimp.pdf) **(Finnish)**

[10] *The Jargon Book*, "Chrome" (http://www.catb.org/~esr/jargon/html/C/chrome.html)

[11] Jakob Nielsen. "Browser and GUI Chrome" (http://www.useit.com/alertbox/ui-chrome.html). .

[12] The ViewTouch restaurant system (http://www.atarimagazines.com/startv2n6/gettingdowntobusiness.html) by Giselle Bisson

[13] Computerhope.com (http://www.computerhope.com/issues/ch000619.htm)

[14] Technet.com (http://blogs.technet.com/mscom/archive/2007/03/12/the-gui-versus-the-command-line-which-is-better-part-1.aspx)

[15] *Macworld.com* November 11, 2006. Dan Moren. CES Unveiled@NY '07: Point and click coming to set-top boxes? (http://gadgets.macworld.com/video/ces_unveiledny_07_point_and_cl.php)

External links

- The men who really invented the GUI (http://www.pcw.co.uk/personal-computer-world/features/2045763/men-really-invented-gui) by Clive Akass
- Graphical User Interface Gallery (http://toastytech.com/guis/index.html), screenshots of various GUIs
- Marcin Wichary's GUIdebook (http://www.guidebookgallery.org/), Graphical User Interface gallery: over 5500 screenshots of GUI, application and icon history
- The Real History of the GUI (http://articles.sitepoint.com/article/real-history-gui) by Mike Tuck
- A History of the GUI (http://arstechnica.com/old/content/2005/05/gui.ars) by Jeremy Reimer of Ars Technica
- In The Beginning Was The Command Line (http://www.nealstephenson.com/command/) by Neal Stephenson

Web_browser

A **web browser** is a software application for retrieving, presenting, and traversing information resources on the World Wide Web. An *information resource* is identified by a Uniform Resource Identifier (URI) and may be a web page, image, video, or other piece of content.[1] Hyperlinks present in resources enable users easily to navigate their browsers to related resources. A web browser can also be defined as an application software or program designed to enable users to access, retrieve and view documents and other resources on the Internet.

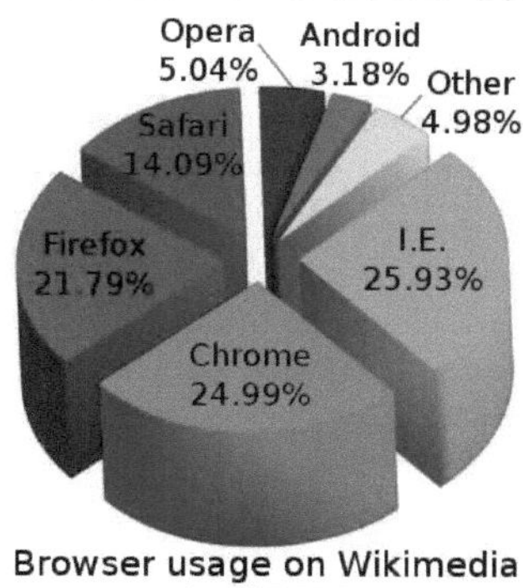

Web browser usage on Wikimedia servers

Although browsers are primarily intended to access the World Wide Web, they can also be used to access information provided by web servers in private networks or files in file systems. The major web browsers are Firefox, Google Chrome, Internet Explorer, Opera, and Safari.[2]

History

The first web browser was invented in 1990 by Sir Tim Berners-Lee. It was called WorldWideWeb (no spaces) and was later renamed Nexus.[4]

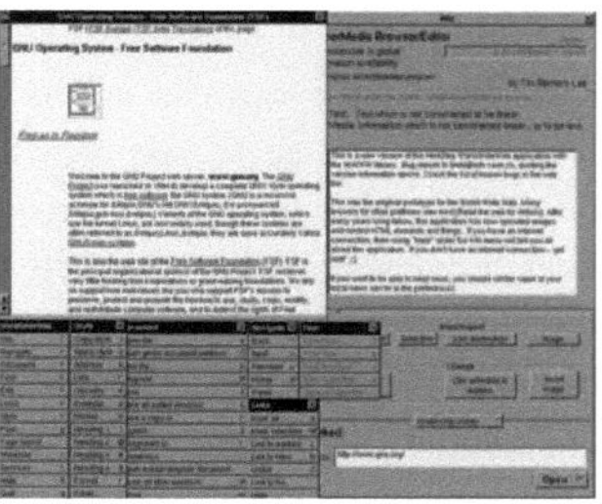
WorldWideWeb for NeXT, released in 1991, was the first web browser.[3]

In 1993, browser software was further innovated by Marc Andreessen with the release of Mosaic (later Netscape), "the world's first popular browser",[5] which made the World Wide Web system easy to use and more accessible to the average person. Andreesen's browser sparked the internet boom of the 1990s.[5] The introduction of Mosaic in 1993 – one of the first graphical web browsers – led to an explosion in web use. Andreessen, the leader of the Mosaic team at NCSA, soon started his own company, named Netscape, and released the Mosaic-influenced Netscape Navigator in 1994, which quickly became the world's most popular browser, accounting for 90% of all web use at its peak (see usage share of web browsers).

Marc Andreessen

Microsoft responded with its Internet Explorer in 1995, also heavily influenced by Mosaic, initiating the industry's first browser war. Bundled with Windows, Internet Explorer gained dominance in the web browser market; Internet Explorer usage share peaked at over 95% by 2002.[6]

Opera debuted in 1996; although it has never achieved widespread use, having less than 2% browser usage share as of February 2012 according to Net Applications.[7] Its Opera-mini version has an additive share, in April 2011 amounting to 1.1% of overall browser use, but focused on the fast-growing mobile phone web browser market, being preinstalled on over 40 million phones. It is also available on several other embedded systems, including Nintendo's Wii video game console.

In 1998, Netscape launched what was to become the Mozilla Foundation in an attempt to produce a competitive browser using the open source software model. That browser would eventually evolve into Firefox, which developed a respectable following while still in the beta stage of development; shortly after the release of Firefox 1.0 in late 2004, Firefox (all versions) accounted for 7% of browser use.[6] As of August 2011, Firefox has a 28% usage share.[7]

Apple's Safari had its first beta release in January 2003; as of April 2011, it had a dominant share of Apple-based web browsing, accounting for just over 7% of the entire browser market.[7]

The most recent major entrant to the browser market is Google's Chrome, first released in September 2008. Chrome's take-up has increased significantly year on year, by doubling its usage share from 8% to 16% by August 2011. This increase seems largely to be at the expense of Internet Explorer, whose share has tended to decrease from month to month.[8] In December 2011, However, when all versions of Internet Explorer are put together, IE is still most popular.[9]

Function

The primary purpose of a web browser is to bring information resources to the user. This process begins when the user inputs a Uniform Resource Locator (URL), for example *http://en.wikipedia.org/*, into the browser. The prefix of the URL, the Uniform Resource Identifier or URI, determines how the URL will be interpreted. The most commonly used kind of URI starts with *http:* and identifies a resource to be retrieved over the Hypertext Transfer Protocol (HTTP). Many browsers also support a variety of other prefixes, such as *https:* for HTTPS, *ftp:* for the File Transfer Protocol, and *file:* for local files. Prefixes that the web browser cannot directly handle are often handed off to another application entirely. For example, *mailto:* URIs are usually passed to the user's default e-mail application, and *news:* URIs are passed to the user's default newsgroup reader.

In the case of *http*, *https*, *file*, and others, once the resource has been retrieved the web browser will display it. HTML is passed to the browser's layout engine to be transformed from markup to an interactive document. Aside from HTML, web browsers can generally display any kind of content that can be part of a web page. Most browsers can display images, audio, video, and XML files, and often have plug-ins to support Flash applications and Java applets. Upon encountering a file of an unsupported type or a file that is set up to be downloaded rather than displayed, the browser prompts the user to save the file to disk.

Information resources may contain hyperlinks to other information resources. Each link contains the URI of a resource to go to. When a link is clicked, the browser navigates to the resource indicated by the link's target URI, and the process of bringing content to the user begins again.

Features

Available web browsers range in features from minimal, text-based user interfaces with bare-bones support for HTML to rich user interfaces supporting a wide variety of file formats and protocols. Browsers which include additional components to support e-mail, Usenet news, and Internet Relay Chat (IRC), are sometimes referred to as "Internet suites" rather than merely "web browsers".[10] [11] [12]

All major web browsers allow the user to open multiple information resources at the same time, either in different browser windows or in different tabs of the same window. Major browsers also include pop-up blockers to prevent unwanted windows from "popping up" without the user's consent.[13] [14] [15] [16]

Most web browsers can display a list of web pages that the user has *bookmarked* so that the user can quickly return to them. Bookmarks are also called "Favorites" in Internet Explorer. In addition, all major web browsers have some form of built-in web feed aggregator. In Firefox, web feeds are formatted as "live bookmarks" and behave like a folder of bookmarks corresponding to recent entries in the feed.[17] In Opera, a more traditional feed reader is included which stores and displays the contents of the feed.[18]

Furthermore, most browsers can be extended via plug-ins, downloadable components that provide additional features.

User interface

Most major web browsers have these user interface elements in common:[19]

- *Back* and *forward* buttons to go back to the previous resource and forward respectively.
- A *refresh* or *reload* button to reload the current resource.
- A *stop* button to cancel loading the resource. In some browsers, the stop button is merged with the reload button.
- A *home* button to return to the user's home page.
- An address bar to input the Uniform Resource Identifier (URI) of the desired resource and display it.
- A search bar to input terms into a search engine. In some browsers, the search bar is merged with the address bar.
- A status bar to display progress in loading the resource and also the URI of links when the cursor hovers over them, and page zooming capability.

Major browsers also possess incremental find features to search within a web page.

Privacy and security

Most browsers support HTTP Secure and offer quick and easy ways to delete the web cache, cookies, and browsing history. For a comparison of the current security vulnerabilities of browsers, see comparison of web browsers.Browsers should also be very secure, as malware is a constant threat on the internet.

Standards support

Early web browsers supported only a very simple version of HTML. The rapid development of proprietary web browsers led to the development of non-standard dialects of HTML, leading to problems with interoperability. Modern web browsers support a combination of standards-based and *de facto* HTML and XHTML, which should be rendered in the same way by all browsers.

Extensibility

A browser extension is a computer program that extends the functionality of a web browser. Every major web browser supports the development of browser extensions.

See also

- Geobrowsing
- List of web browsers
- Mobile browser
- Timeline of web browsers
- Web browser history

References

[1] Jacobs, Ian; Walsh, Norman (15 December 2004). "URI/Resource Relationships" (http://www.w3.org/TR/webarch/#id-resources). *Architecture of the World Wide Web, Volume One*. World Wide Web Consortium. . Retrieved 30 June 2009.

[2] "Browser" (http://mashable.com/follow/topics/browser/). Mashable. . Retrieved September 2, 2011.

[3] Stewart, William. "Web Browser History" (http://www.livinginternet.com/w/wi_browse.htm). . Retrieved 5 May 2009.

[4] "Tim Berners-Lee: WorldWideWeb, the first Web client" (http://www.w3.org/People/Berners-Lee/WorldWideWeb.html). W3.org. . Retrieved 2011-12-07.

[5] "Bloomberg Game Changers: Marc Andreesen" (http://www.bloomberg.com/video/67758394). Bloomberg.com. 2011-03-17. . Retrieved 2011-12-07.

[6] November 24, 2004 (2004-11-24). "Mozilla Firefox Internet Browser Market Share Gains to 7.4%" (http://www.searchenginejournal.com/mozilla-firefox-internet-browser-market-share-gains-to-74/1082/). Search Engine Journal. . Retrieved 2011-12-07.

[7] http://gs.statcounter.com/#browser-ww-monthly-201108-201108-bar

[8] "Internet Explorer usage to plummet below 50 percent by mid-2012" (http://www.digitaltrends.com/web/internet-explorer-usage-to-plummet-below-50-percent-by-mid-2012/attachment/net-applications-browser-market/). September 3, 2011. . Retrieved September 4, 2011.

[9] "CNN Money claims that Chrome is more popular than IE8" (http://money.cnn.com/2011/12/16/technology/chrome_internet_explorer/?source=cnn_bin). CNN. . Retrieved December 19, 2011.

[10] "The SeaMonkey Project" (http://www.seamonkey-project.org/). Mozilla Foundation. 7 November 2008. . Retrieved 30 June 2009.

[11] "Cyberdog: Welcome to the 'doghouse!" (http://www.cyberdog.org/). 5 July 2009. . Retrieved 30 June 2009.

[12] Teelucksingh, Dev Anand. "Interesting DOS programs" (http://www.opus.co.tt/dave/internet.htm). Opus Networkx. . Retrieved 30 June 2009.

[13] Andersen, Starr; Abella, Vincent (15 September 2004). "Part 5: Enhanced Browsing Security" (http://technet.microsoft.com/en-us/library/bb457150.aspx#EEAA). *Changes to Functionality in Microsoft Windows XP Service Pack 2*. Microsoft. . Retrieved 30 June 2009.

[14] "Pop-up blocker" (http://support.mozilla.com/en-US/kb/Pop-up+blocker). Mozilla Foundation. . Retrieved 30 June 2009.

[15] "Safari: Using The Pop-Up Blocker" (http://www.mactipsandtricks.com/tips/display.lasso?mactip=137). *Mac Tips and Tricks*. WeHostMacs. 2004. . Retrieved 30 June 2009.

[16] "Simple settings" (http://www.opera.com/browser/tutorials/settings/#tabs). *Opera Tutorials*. Opera Software. . Retrieved 30 June 2009.

[17] Bokma, John. "Mozilla Firefox: RSS and Live Bookmarks" (http://johnbokma.com/firefox/rss-and-live-bookmarks.html). . Retrieved 30 June 2009.

[18] "RSS newsfeeds in Opera Mail" (http://www.opera.com/mail/rss/). Opera Software. . Retrieved 30 June 2009.

[19] "About Browsers and their Features" (http://www.about-the-web.com/shtml/browsers.shtml). SpiritWorks Software Development. . Retrieved 5 May 2009.

External links

- Architecture of the World Wide Web, Volume One (http://www.w3.org/TR/webarch/)
- Existing browsers (http://www.browserchoice.eu/BrowserChoice/browserchoice_en.htm)
- WorldWideWeb: Proposal for a HyperText Project (http://www.w3.org/Proposal.html)

Text_mode

Text mode is a kind of computer display mode in which the content of the screen is internally represented in terms of characters rather than individual pixels. Typically, the screen consists of a uniform rectangular grid of *character cells*, each of which contains one of the characters of a character set. Text mode is contrasted to all points addressable (APA) mode or other kinds of computer graphics modes.

Text mode video rendering came to prominence in the early 1970s, when video-oriented text terminals started to replace teleprinters in the interactive use of computers.

Text mode applications communicate with the user with command-line interfaces and text user interfaces. Many character sets used in text mode applications also contain a limited set of predefined semi-graphical characters usable for drawing boxes, and other rudimentary graphics which can be used to highlight the content or to simulate widget or control interface objects found in GUI programs. A typical example is the IBM code page 437 character set.

An important characteristic of text mode programs is that they assume monospace fonts, where every character has the same width on screen, which allows to easily maintain the vertical alignment when displaying semi-graphical characters. This was an analogy of early mechanical printers which had fixed pitch (teleprinters and daisy wheel printers, etc.). This way, the output seen on the screen could be sent directly to the printer maintaining exactly the same format.

Depending on the environment, the screen buffer can be directly addressable. Programs that display output on remote video terminals must issue special control sequences to manipulate the screen buffer. The most popular standards for such control sequences are ANSI and VT100.

Programs accessing the screen buffer through control sequences may lose synchronization with the actual display, so that many text mode programs have a *redisplay everything* command, often associated with the Ctrl-L key combination.

Advantages and disadvantages

The advantages of text modes as compared to graphics modes include lower memory consumption and faster screen manipulation. At the time text terminals were replacing teleprinters in the 1970s, the extremely high cost of random access memory in that period made it exorbitantly expensive to install enough memory for a computer to simultaneously store the current value of *every* pixel on a screen (the first Macintosh was groundbreaking and very expensive because it attempted to do precisely that). Text mode avoids the problem of expensive memory by having dedicated display hardware re-render each line of text from characters into pixels with *each* scan of the screen by the cathode ray. In turn, the display hardware needs only enough memory to store the pixels equivalent to one line of text (or even less) at a time. Thus, the computer only stores and knows about the underlying text characters (hence the name "text mode") and the only location where the actual pixels representing those characters exist as a single unified image is the screen itself, as viewed by the user.

In addition, text mode applications have relatively low bandwidth requirements in remote terminal use. An obvious disadvantage of text mode is the restricted screen content.

User-defined characters

The border between text mode and graphical programs can sometimes be fuzzy, especially on the PC's VGA hardware, because many later text mode programs tried to push the model to the extreme by playing with the video controller. For example, they redefined the character set in order to create custom semi-graphical characters, or even created the appearance of a graphical mouse by redefining the appearance of the characters over which the mouse was shown at a given time.

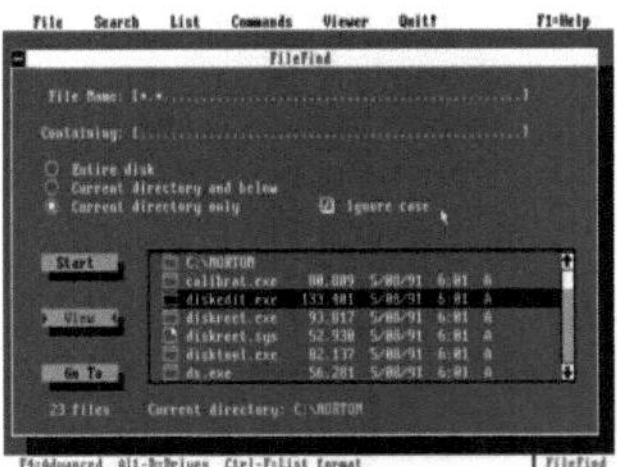

Norton Utilities 6.01, an example of advanced TUI which redefines the character set to show tiny graphical widgets, icons and an arrow pointer in text mode.

Text mode rendering with user-defined characters has also been useful for 2D computer and video games because the game screen can be manipulated much faster than with pixel-oriented rendering.

Technical basis

A video controller implementing a text mode usually uses two distinct areas of memory. *Character memory* or a *pattern table* contains a raster font in use, where each character is represented by a dot matrix (a matrix of bits), so the character memory could be considered as a three-dimensional bit array. *Display matrix* (a *text buffer*, *screen buffer*, or *nametable*) tracks which character is in each cell. In the simple case the display matrix can be just a matrix of code points (so named *character pointer table*), but it usually stores for each character position not only a code, but also *attributes*.

L\C	0 0 0 0 0	0 0 0 0 1	0 0 0 1 0	0 0 0 1 1	0 0 1 0 0	0 0 1 0 1	0 0 1 1 0	0 0 1 1 1	00000000 11111111 00001111 00110011 01010101	11... 00... 00... 00... 01...
00000		■	■	■	■	■				
00001	■	■				■	■			
00010	■	■		■	■	■	■			
00011	■	■		■	■	■	■			
00100	■	■		■	■	■	■			
00101	■	■								
00110		■	■	■	■					
00111										
01000 01001 ...	... ...									

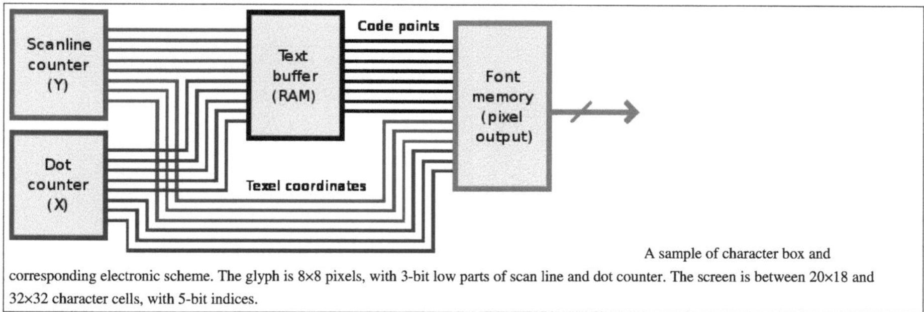

A sample of character box and corresponding electronic scheme. The glyph is 8×8 pixels, with 3-bit low parts of scan line and dot counter. The screen is between 20×18 and 32×32 character cells, with 5-bit indices.

In the case of raster scan output, which is the most common for computer monitors, the corresponding video signal is made by the *character generator*, a special electronic unit similar to devices with the same name used in video technology. The video controller has two registers: scan line counter and dot counter, serving as coordinates in the screen dot matrix. Each of them must be divided by corresponding glyph size to obtain an index in the display matrix; the remainder is an index in glyph matrix. If glyph size equals to 2^n, then it is possible just to use n low bits of a binary register as an index in glyph matrix, and the rest of bits as an index in the display matrix — see the scheme.

The character memory resides in a read-only memory in some systems. Other systems allow the use of RAM for this purpose, making it possible to redefine the typeface and even the character set for application-specific purposes. The use of RAM-based characters also facilitates some special techniques, such as the implementation of a pixel-graphics frame buffer by reserving some characters for a bitmap and writing pixels directly to their corresponding character memory. In some historical graphics chips, including the TMS9918, the MOS Technology VIC, and the Game Boy graphics hardware, this was actually the canonical way of doing pixel graphics.

Text modes often assign *attributes* to the displayed characters. For example, the VT100 terminal allows each character to be underlined, brightened, blinking or inverse. Color-supporting devices usually allow the color of each character, and often the background color as well, to be selected from a limited palette of colors. These attributes can either coexist with the character indices or use a different memory area called *color memory* or *attribute memory*.

Some text mode implementations also have the concept of line attributes. For example, the VT100-compatible line of text terminals supports the doubling of the width and height of the characters on individual text lines.

PC common text modes

Depending on the graphics adapter used, a variety of text modes are available on IBM PC compatible computers. They are listed on the table below:

Text res.	Char. size	Graphics res.	Colors	Adapters
80×25	9×14	720×350	B&W Text	MDA, Hercules
40×25	8×8	320×200	16 colors	CGA, EGA
80×25	8×8	640×200	16 colors	CGA, EGA
80×25	8×14	640×350	16 colors	EGA
80×43	8×8	640×350	16 colors	EGA
80×25	9×16	720×400	16 colors	VGA
80×30	8×16	640×480	16 colors	VGA
80×50	9×8	720×400	16 colors	VGA

80×60			16 colors	VESA-compatible Super VGA
132×25			16 colors	VESA-compatible Super VGA
132×43			16 colors	VESA-compatible Super VGA
132×50			16 colors	VESA-compatible Super VGA
132×60			16 colors	VESA-compatible Super VGA

MDA text could be emphasized with bright, underline, reverse and blinking attributes.

Video cards in general are backward compatible, i.e. EGA supports all MDA and CGA modes, VGA supports MDA, CGA and EGA modes.

By far the most common text mode used in DOS environments, and initial Windows consoles, is the default 80 columns by 25 rows, or 80×25, with 16 colors. This mode was available on practically all IBM and compatible personal computers. Several programs, such as terminal emulators, used only 80×24 for the main display and reserved the bottom row for a status bar.

Two other VGA text modes, 90×43 and 90×50, exist but were very rarely used. The 40-column text modes were never very popular outside games and other applications designed for compatibility with television monitors, and were used only for demonstration purposes or with very old hardware.

Character sizes and graphical resolutions for the extended VESA-compatible Super VGA text modes are manufacturer-dependent. Also on these display adapters, available colors can be halved from 16 to 8 when a second customized character set is employed (giving a total repertoire of 512 —instead the common 256— different graphic characters simultaneously displayed on the screen).

Some cards (e.g. S3) supported custom very large text modes, like 100×37 or even 160×120. In Linux systems, a program called SVGATextMode is often used with SVGA cards to set up very large console text modes.

Modern usage

Many modern programs with a graphical interface simulate the display style of text mode programs, notably when it is important to preserve the vertical alignment of text, e.g., during computer programming. There exist also software components to emulate text mode, such as terminal emulators or command line consoles. In Microsoft Windows, the Win32 console usually opens in emulated, graphical window mode it can be switched to full screen, true text mode and vice versa by pressing the Alt and Enter keys together (this is no longer supported in Windows 7).

Linux virtual console operates in text mode. Most Linux distributions support several virtual console screens, accessed by pressing Ctrl, Alt and a function key together.

See also

- Text user interface
- Text mode demos — computer animations generated in text mode
- Teletext
- Text semigraphics
- ASCII art
- Twin
- Code page 437

External links

- High-Resolution console on Linux [1]

References

[1] http://www.digitalhermit.com/linux/hiresconsole.html

Keyboard_shortcut

In computing, a **keyboard shortcut** is a finite set of one or more keys that invoke a software or operating system operation when triggered by the user. A meaning of term "keyboard shortcut" can vary depending on software manufacturer. For instance, Microsoft differentiates keyboard shortcuts from **hotkeys** (mnemonics) whereby the former consists of a specific key combination used to trigger an action, and the latter represents a designated letter in a menu command or toolbar button that when pressed together with the Alt key, activates such command.

Firefox 3.0 menu with shortcuts highlighted with green and mnemonics highlighted with yellow.

Description

Keyboard shortcuts are typically an alternate means for invoking one or more commands that would otherwise be accessible only through a menu, a pointing device, different levels of a user interface, or via a command console. Keyboard shortcuts generally expedite common operations by reducing input sequences to a few keystrokes, hence the term "shortcut".[1]

Some keyboard shortcuts require the user to press a single key or a sequence of keys one after the other. Other keyboard shortcuts require pressing and holding several keys simultaneously. For simultaneous keyboard shortcuts, one usually first holds down the modifier key(s), then quickly presses and releases the regular (non-modifier) key, and finally releases the modifier key(s). This distinction is important, as trying to press all the keys simultaneously will frequently either miss some of the modifier keys, or cause unwanted auto-repeat. One exception is shortcuts involving the <kbd class="keyboard-key nowrap" style="border: 1px solid #aaa; -moz-border-radius: 2px; -webkit-border-radius: 2px; border-radius: 2px; -moz-box-shadow: 1px 2px 2px #ddd; -webkit-box-shadow: 1px 2px 2px #ddd; box-shadow: 1px 2px 2px #ddd; background-color: #f9f9f9; background-image: -moz-linear-gradient(top, #eee, #f9f9f9, #eee); background-image: -ms-linear-gradient(top, #eee, #f9f9f9, #eee); background-image: -o-linear-gradient(top, #eee, #f9f9f9, #eee); background-image: -webkit-linear-gradient(top, #eee, #f9f9f9, #eee); background-image: linear-gradient(top, #eee, #f9f9f9, #eee); padding: 1px 3px; font-family: inherit; font-size: 0.85em;">Esc</kbd> key, which almost always requires pressing and releasing the Esc key before pressing the next key.

Mnemonics are distinguishable from keyboard shortcuts. One difference between them is that the keyboard shortcuts are not localized on multi-language software but the mnemonics are generally localized to reflect the symbols and letters used in the specific locale. In most GUIs, a program's keyboard shortcuts are discoverable by browsing the program's menus - the shortcut is indicated in the menu choice. There are keyboards, commonly called Specialty Keyboards that have the shortcuts for a particular application already marked on them. These keyboards can help the users learn the shortcuts and improve their speed of using the particular applications. In certain cases, those keyboards can be created by applying shortcut stickers on a regular keyboard, which usually gives quicker access to software program features not visible otherwise. Such keyboards are often used for editing video, audio, or graphics,[2] as well as in software training courses.

Customization

When shortcuts are referred to as **key bindings** it carries the connotation that the shortcuts are customizable to a user's preference and that program functions may be 'bound' to a different set of keystrokes instead of or in addition to the default. This highlights a difference in philosophy regarding shortcuts. Some systems, typically end-user-oriented systems such as Windows or Macintosh consider standardized shortcuts essential to the environment's ease of use. These systems usually limit a user's ability to change shortcuts, typically requiring a separate, possibly third-party, utility to perform the task. Other systems, typically Unix and related, consider shortcuts to be a user's prerogative, and that they should be changeable to suit individual preference. Hardcore gamers often customize their key bindings in order to increase performance via faster reaction times. In most real-world environments, both philosophies co-exist; a core set of *sacred* shortcuts remain fixed while others, typically involving an otherwise unused modifier key or keys, are under the user's control.

"Sacred" keybindings

The original Macintosh interface defined a set of keyboard shortcuts that would remain consistent across application programs. This provides a better user experience than the situation then prevalent of applications using wholly unrelated keys for different functions. This could result in data loss under multitasking systems if, for example, one program used -D to mean "Delete" while another used it to access a "Disk" menu. The standard bindings were:

- <kbd class="keyboard-key nowrap" style="border: 1px solid #aaa; -moz-border-radius: 2px; -webkit-border-radius: 2px; border-radius: 2px; -moz-box-shadow: 1px 2px 2px #ddd; -webkit-box-shadow: 1px 2px 2px #ddd; box-shadow: 1px 2px 2px #ddd; background-color: #f9f9f9; background-image: -moz-linear-gradient(top, #eee, #f9f9f9, #eee); background-image: -ms-linear-gradient(top, #eee, #f9f9f9, #eee); background-image: -o-linear-gradient(top, #eee, #f9f9f9, #eee); background-image: -webkit-linear-gradient(top, #eee, #f9f9f9, #eee); background-image: linear-gradient(top, #eee, #f9f9f9, #eee); padding: 1px 3px; font-family: inherit; font-size: 0.85em;">Q</kbd> : **Q**uit
- <kbd class="keyboard-key nowrap" style="border: 1px solid #aaa; -moz-border-radius: 2px; -webkit-border-radius: 2px; border-radius: 2px; -moz-box-shadow: 1px 2px 2px #ddd; -webkit-box-shadow: 1px 2px 2px #ddd; box-shadow: 1px 2px 2px #ddd; background-color: #f9f9f9; background-image: -moz-linear-gradient(top, #eee, #f9f9f9, #eee); background-image: -ms-linear-gradient(top, #eee, #f9f9f9, #eee); background-image: -o-linear-gradient(top, #eee, #f9f9f9, #eee); background-image: -webkit-linear-gradient(top, #eee, #f9f9f9, #eee); background-image: linear-gradient(top, #eee, #f9f9f9, #eee); padding: 1px 3px; font-family: inherit; font-size: 0.85em;">W</kbd> : Close **W**indow
- <kbd class="keyboard-key nowrap" style="border: 1px solid #aaa; -moz-border-radius: 2px; -webkit-border-radius: 2px; border-radius: 2px; -moz-box-shadow: 1px 2px 2px #ddd; -webkit-box-shadow: 1px 2px 2px #ddd; box-shadow: 1px 2px 2px #ddd; background-color: #f9f9f9; background-image: -moz-linear-gradient(top, #eee, #f9f9f9, #eee); background-image: -ms-linear-gradient(top, #eee, #f9f9f9, #eee); background-image: -o-linear-gradient(top, #eee, #f9f9f9, #eee); background-image: -webkit-linear-gradient(top,

#eee, #f9f9f9, #eee); background-image: linear-gradient(top, #eee, #f9f9f9, #eee); padding: 1px 3px; font-family: inherit; font-size: 0.85em;">I</kbd> : **I**talicize text

- <kbd class="keyboard-key nowrap" style="border: 1px solid #aaa; -moz-border-radius: 2px; -webkit-border-radius: 2px; border-radius: 2px; -moz-box-shadow: 1px 2px 2px #ddd; -webkit-box-shadow: 1px 2px 2px #ddd; box-shadow: 1px 2px 2px #ddd; background-color: #f9f9f9; background-image: -moz-linear-gradient(top, #eee, #f9f9f9, #eee); background-image: -ms-linear-gradient(top, #eee, #f9f9f9, #eee); background-image: -o-linear-gradient(top, #eee, #f9f9f9, #eee); background-image: -webkit-linear-gradient(top, #eee, #f9f9f9, #eee); background-image: linear-gradient(top, #eee, #f9f9f9, #eee); padding: 1px 3px; font-family: inherit; font-size: 0.85em;">U</kbd> : **U**nderline text
- <kbd class="keyboard-key nowrap" style="border: 1px solid #aaa; -moz-border-radius: 2px; -webkit-border-radius: 2px; border-radius: 2px; -moz-box-shadow: 1px 2px 2px #ddd; -webkit-box-shadow: 1px 2px 2px #ddd; box-shadow: 1px 2px 2px #ddd; background-color: #f9f9f9; background-image: -moz-linear-gradient(top, #eee, #f9f9f9, #eee); background-image: -ms-linear-gradient(top, #eee, #f9f9f9, #eee); background-image: -o-linear-gradient(top, #eee, #f9f9f9, #eee); background-image: -webkit-linear-gradient(top, #eee, #f9f9f9, #eee); background-image: linear-gradient(top, #eee, #f9f9f9, #eee); padding: 1px 3px; font-family: inherit; font-size: 0.85em;">O</kbd> : **O**pen
- <kbd class="keyboard-key nowrap" style="border: 1px solid #aaa; -moz-border-radius: 2px; -webkit-border-radius: 2px; border-radius: 2px; -moz-box-shadow: 1px 2px 2px #ddd; -webkit-box-shadow: 1px 2px 2px #ddd; box-shadow: 1px 2px 2px #ddd; background-color: #f9f9f9; background-image: -moz-linear-gradient(top, #eee, #f9f9f9, #eee); background-image: -ms-linear-gradient(top, #eee, #f9f9f9, #eee); background-image: -o-linear-gradient(top, #eee, #f9f9f9, #eee); background-image: -webkit-linear-gradient(top, #eee, #f9f9f9, #eee); background-image: linear-gradient(top, #eee, #f9f9f9, #eee); padding: 1px 3px; font-family: inherit; font-size: 0.85em;">P</kbd> : **P**rint
- <kbd class="keyboard-key nowrap" style="border: 1px solid #aaa; -moz-border-radius: 2px; -webkit-border-radius: 2px; border-radius: 2px; -moz-box-shadow: 1px 2px 2px #ddd; -webkit-box-shadow: 1px 2px 2px #ddd; box-shadow: 1px 2px 2px #ddd; background-color: #f9f9f9; background-image: -moz-linear-gradient(top, #eee, #f9f9f9, #eee); background-image: -ms-linear-gradient(top, #eee, #f9f9f9, #eee); background-image: -o-linear-gradient(top, #eee, #f9f9f9, #eee); background-image: -webkit-linear-gradient(top, #eee, #f9f9f9, #eee); background-image: linear-gradient(top, #eee, #f9f9f9, #eee); padding: 1px 3px; font-family: inherit; font-size: 0.85em;">A</kbd> : Select **A**ll
- <kbd class="keyboard-key nowrap" style="border: 1px solid #aaa; -moz-border-radius: 2px; -webkit-border-radius: 2px; border-radius: 2px; -moz-box-shadow: 1px 2px 2px #ddd; -webkit-box-shadow: 1px 2px 2px #ddd; box-shadow: 1px 2px 2px #ddd; background-color: #f9f9f9; background-image: -moz-linear-gradient(top, #eee, #f9f9f9, #eee); background-image: -ms-linear-gradient(top, #eee, #f9f9f9, #eee); background-image: -o-linear-gradient(top, #eee, #f9f9f9, #eee); background-image: -webkit-linear-gradient(top, #eee, #f9f9f9, #eee); background-image: linear-gradient(top, #eee, #f9f9f9, #eee); padding: 1px 3px; font-family: inherit; font-size: 0.85em;">S</kbd> : **S**ave
- <kbd class="keyboard-key nowrap" style="border: 1px solid #aaa; -moz-border-radius: 2px; -webkit-border-radius: 2px; border-radius: 2px; -moz-box-shadow: 1px 2px 2px #ddd; -webkit-box-shadow: 1px 2px 2px #ddd; box-shadow: 1px 2px 2px #ddd; background-color: #f9f9f9; background-image: -moz-linear-gradient(top, #eee, #f9f9f9, #eee); background-image: -ms-linear-gradient(top, #eee, #f9f9f9, #eee); background-image: -o-linear-gradient(top, #eee, #f9f9f9, #eee); background-image: -webkit-linear-gradient(top, #eee, #f9f9f9, #eee); background-image: linear-gradient(top, #eee, #f9f9f9, #eee); padding: 1px 3px; font-family: inherit; font-size: 0.85em;">F</kbd> : **F**ind
- <kbd class="keyboard-key nowrap" style="border: 1px solid #aaa; -moz-border-radius: 2px; -webkit-border-radius: 2px; border-radius: 2px; -moz-box-shadow: 1px 2px 2px #ddd; -webkit-box-shadow: 1px 2px 2px #ddd; box-shadow: 1px 2px 2px #ddd; background-color: #f9f9f9; background-image:

-moz-linear-gradient(top, #eee, #f9f9f9, #eee); background-image: -ms-linear-gradient(top, #eee, #f9f9f9, #eee); background-image: -o-linear-gradient(top, #eee, #f9f9f9, #eee); background-image: -webkit-linear-gradient(top, #eee, #f9f9f9, #eee); background-image: linear-gradient(top, #eee, #f9f9f9, #eee); padding: 1px 3px; font-family: inherit; font-size: 0.85em;">Z</kbd> : Undo (resembles the action of striking out a mistake)

- <kbd class="keyboard-key nowrap" style="border: 1px solid #aaa; -moz-border-radius: 2px; -webkit-border-radius: 2px; border-radius: 2px; -moz-box-shadow: 1px 2px 2px #ddd; -webkit-box-shadow: 1px 2px 2px #ddd; box-shadow: 1px 2px 2px #ddd; background-color: #f9f9f9; background-image: -moz-linear-gradient(top, #eee, #f9f9f9, #eee); background-image: -ms-linear-gradient(top, #eee, #f9f9f9, #eee); background-image: -o-linear-gradient(top, #eee, #f9f9f9, #eee); background-image: -webkit-linear-gradient(top, #eee, #f9f9f9, #eee); background-image: linear-gradient(top, #eee, #f9f9f9, #eee); padding: 1px 3px; font-family: inherit; font-size: 0.85em;">X</kbd> : Cut (resembles scissors)
- <kbd class="keyboard-key nowrap" style="border: 1px solid #aaa; -moz-border-radius: 2px; -webkit-border-radius: 2px; border-radius: 2px; -moz-box-shadow: 1px 2px 2px #ddd; -webkit-box-shadow: 1px 2px 2px #ddd; box-shadow: 1px 2px 2px #ddd; background-color: #f9f9f9; background-image: -moz-linear-gradient(top, #eee, #f9f9f9, #eee); background-image: -ms-linear-gradient(top, #eee, #f9f9f9, #eee); background-image: -o-linear-gradient(top, #eee, #f9f9f9, #eee); background-image: -webkit-linear-gradient(top, #eee, #f9f9f9, #eee); background-image: linear-gradient(top, #eee, #f9f9f9, #eee); padding: 1px 3px; font-family: inherit; font-size: 0.85em;">C</kbd> : **C**opy
- <kbd class="keyboard-key nowrap" style="border: 1px solid #aaa; -moz-border-radius: 2px; -webkit-border-radius: 2px; border-radius: 2px; -moz-box-shadow: 1px 2px 2px #ddd; -webkit-box-shadow: 1px 2px 2px #ddd; box-shadow: 1px 2px 2px #ddd; background-color: #f9f9f9; background-image: -moz-linear-gradient(top, #eee, #f9f9f9, #eee); background-image: -ms-linear-gradient(top, #eee, #f9f9f9, #eee); background-image: -o-linear-gradient(top, #eee, #f9f9f9, #eee); background-image: -webkit-linear-gradient(top, #eee, #f9f9f9, #eee); background-image: linear-gradient(top, #eee, #f9f9f9, #eee); padding: 1px 3px; font-family: inherit; font-size: 0.85em;">V</kbd> : Paste (resembles an arrow pointing downward "into" the document, or a brush used for applying paste)
- <kbd class="keyboard-key nowrap" style="border: 1px solid #aaa; -moz-border-radius: 2px; -webkit-border-radius: 2px; border-radius: 2px; -moz-box-shadow: 1px 2px 2px #ddd; -webkit-box-shadow: 1px 2px 2px #ddd; box-shadow: 1px 2px 2px #ddd; background-color: #f9f9f9; background-image: -moz-linear-gradient(top, #eee, #f9f9f9, #eee); background-image: -ms-linear-gradient(top, #eee, #f9f9f9, #eee); background-image: -o-linear-gradient(top, #eee, #f9f9f9, #eee); background-image: -webkit-linear-gradient(top, #eee, #f9f9f9, #eee); background-image: linear-gradient(top, #eee, #f9f9f9, #eee); padding: 1px 3px; font-family: inherit; font-size: 0.85em;">B</kbd> : **B**old text
- <kbd class="keyboard-key nowrap" style="border: 1px solid #aaa; -moz-border-radius: 2px; -webkit-border-radius: 2px; border-radius: 2px; -moz-box-shadow: 1px 2px 2px #ddd; -webkit-box-shadow: 1px 2px 2px #ddd; box-shadow: 1px 2px 2px #ddd; background-color: #f9f9f9; background-image: -moz-linear-gradient(top, #eee, #f9f9f9, #eee); background-image: -ms-linear-gradient(top, #eee, #f9f9f9, #eee); background-image: -o-linear-gradient(top, #eee, #f9f9f9, #eee); background-image: -webkit-linear-gradient(top, #eee, #f9f9f9, #eee); background-image: linear-gradient(top, #eee, #f9f9f9, #eee); padding: 1px 3px; font-family: inherit; font-size: 0.85em;">N</kbd> : **N**ew Document
- <kbd class="keyboard-key nowrap" style="border: 1px solid #aaa; -moz-border-radius: 2px; -webkit-border-radius: 2px; border-radius: 2px; -moz-box-shadow: 1px 2px 2px #ddd; -webkit-box-shadow: 1px 2px 2px #ddd; box-shadow: 1px 2px 2px #ddd; background-color: #f9f9f9; background-image: -moz-linear-gradient(top, #eee, #f9f9f9, #eee); background-image: -ms-linear-gradient(top, #eee, #f9f9f9, #eee); background-image: -o-linear-gradient(top, #eee, #f9f9f9, #eee); background-image: -webkit-linear-gradient(top, #eee, #f9f9f9, #eee); background-image: linear-gradient(top, #eee, #f9f9f9, #eee); padding: 1px 3px; font-family: inherit; font-size: 0.85em;">.</kbd> : User interrupt

- <kbd class="keyboard-key nowrap" style="border: 1px solid #aaa; -moz-border-radius: 2px; -webkit-border-radius: 2px; border-radius: 2px; -moz-box-shadow: 1px 2px 2px #ddd; -webkit-box-shadow: 1px 2px 2px #ddd; box-shadow: 1px 2px 2px #ddd; background-color: #f9f9f9; background-image: -moz-linear-gradient(top, #eee, #f9f9f9, #eee); background-image: -ms-linear-gradient(top, #eee, #f9f9f9, #eee); background-image: -o-linear-gradient(top, #eee, #f9f9f9, #eee); background-image: -webkit-linear-gradient(top, #eee, #f9f9f9, #eee); background-image: linear-gradient(top, #eee, #f9f9f9, #eee); padding: 1px 3px; font-family: inherit; font-size: 0.85em;">?</kbd> : Help (? signifies a question or confusion)

Problems with access keys

In summer 2002 a non-scientific study concluded that various web browsers like the IBM Home Page Reader did not make any distinction between the built in keyboard shortcuts for going in different modes and available access keys in websites.[3]

Notation

The simplest keyboard shortcuts consist of only one key. For these, one generally just writes out the name of the key, as in the message "Press F1 for Help". The name of the key is sometimes surrounded in brackets or similar characters. For example: [F1] or <F1>. The key name may also be set off using special formatting (bold, italic, all caps, etc.)

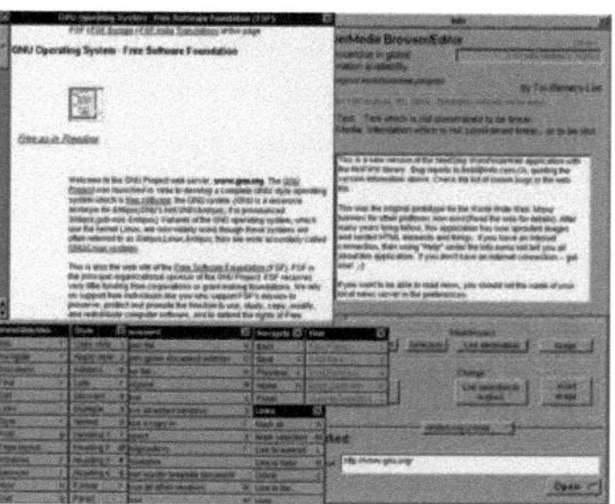

WorldWideWeb for NextStep with keyboard shortcuts visible at bottom left. All shortcuts require the Control key to be pressed. Additionally, the Heading commands under the Style menu and commands under the Link menu require the Shift key to be held down.

Many shortcuts require two or more keys to be pressed together. For these, the usual notation is to list the keys names separated by plus signs or hyphens. For example: "Ctrl+C", "Ctrl-C", or "<kbd class="keyboard-key nowrap" style="border: 1px solid #aaa; -moz-border-radius: 2px; -webkit-border-radius: 2px; border-radius: 2px; -moz-box-shadow: 1px 2px 2px #ddd; -webkit-box-shadow: 1px 2px 2px #ddd; box-shadow: 1px 2px 2px #ddd; background-color: #f9f9f9; background-image: -moz-linear-gradient(top, #eee, #f9f9f9, #eee); background-image: -ms-linear-gradient(top, #eee, #f9f9f9, #eee); background-image: -o-linear-gradient(top, #eee, #f9f9f9, #eee); background-image: -webkit-linear-gradient(top, #eee, #f9f9f9, #eee); background-image: linear-gradient(top, #eee, #f9f9f9, #eee); padding: 1px 3px; font-family: inherit; font-size: 0.85em;">Ctrl</kbd>+<kbd class="keyboard-key nowrap" style="border: 1px solid #aaa; -moz-border-radius: 2px; -webkit-border-radius: 2px; border-radius: 2px; -moz-box-shadow: 1px 2px 2px #ddd; -webkit-box-shadow: 1px 2px 2px #ddd; box-shadow: 1px 2px 2px #ddd; background-color: #f9f9f9; background-image: -moz-linear-gradient(top, #eee, #f9f9f9, #eee); background-image: -ms-linear-gradient(top, #eee, #f9f9f9, #eee); background-image: -o-linear-gradient(top, #eee, #f9f9f9, #eee); background-image: -webkit-linear-gradient(top, #eee, #f9f9f9, #eee); background-image: linear-gradient(top, #eee, #f9f9f9, #eee); padding: 1px 3px; font-family: inherit; font-size: 0.85em;">C</kbd>". The Ctrl key is sometimes indicated by a caret character (^). Thus Ctrl-C is sometimes written as ^C. At times, usually on Unix platforms, the case of the second character is significant - if the character would normally require pressing the Shift key to type, then the Shift key is part of the shortcut e.g. '^C' vs. '^c' or '^@' vs. '^2'.

Some keyboard shortcuts require keys (or sets of keys) to be pressed individually, in sequence. These are generally written with the individual keys (or sets) separated by commas or semicolons. For example "Alt+F, S" or "Alt+F; S" would mean "First press <kbd class="keyboard-key nowrap" style="border: 1px solid #aaa; -moz-border-radius: 2px; -webkit-border-radius: 2px; border-radius: 2px; -moz-box-shadow: 1px 2px 2px #ddd; -webkit-box-shadow: 1px 2px

2px #ddd; box-shadow: 1px 2px 2px #ddd; background-color: #f9f9f9; background-image: -moz-linear-gradient(top, #eee, #f9f9f9, #eee); background-image: -ms-linear-gradient(top, #eee, #f9f9f9, #eee); background-image: -o-linear-gradient(top, #eee, #f9f9f9, #eee); background-image: -webkit-linear-gradient(top, #eee, #f9f9f9, #eee); background-image: linear-gradient(top, #eee, #f9f9f9, #eee); padding: 1px 3px; font-family: inherit; font-size: 0.85em;">Alt</kbd> and <kbd class="keyboard-key nowrap" style="border: 1px solid #aaa; -moz-border-radius: 2px; -webkit-border-radius: 2px; border-radius: 2px; -moz-box-shadow: 1px 2px 2px #ddd; -webkit-box-shadow: 1px 2px 2px #ddd; box-shadow: 1px 2px 2px #ddd; background-color: #f9f9f9; background-image: -moz-linear-gradient(top, #eee, #f9f9f9, #eee); background-image: -ms-linear-gradient(top, #eee, #f9f9f9, #eee); background-image: -o-linear-gradient(top, #eee, #f9f9f9, #eee); background-image: -webkit-linear-gradient(top, #eee, #f9f9f9, #eee); background-image: linear-gradient(top, #eee, #f9f9f9, #eee); padding: 1px 3px; font-family: inherit; font-size: 0.85em;">F</kbd> together, release them and then press <kbd class="keyboard-key nowrap" style="border: 1px solid #aaa; -moz-border-radius: 2px; -webkit-border-radius: 2px; border-radius: 2px; -moz-box-shadow: 1px 2px 2px #ddd; -webkit-box-shadow: 1px 2px 2px #ddd; box-shadow: 1px 2px 2px #ddd; background-color: #f9f9f9; background-image: -moz-linear-gradient(top, #eee, #f9f9f9, #eee); background-image: -ms-linear-gradient(top, #eee, #f9f9f9, #eee); background-image: -o-linear-gradient(top, #eee, #f9f9f9, #eee); background-image: -webkit-linear-gradient(top, #eee, #f9f9f9, #eee); background-image: linear-gradient(top, #eee, #f9f9f9, #eee); padding: 1px 3px; font-family: inherit; font-size: 0.85em;">S</kbd>". Such shortcuts often represent a series of smaller shortcuts, strung together to create a larger action. To continue the "Alt+F, S" example, in many programs, this will open the "File" menu, and then invoke the "Save" function.

See also

- Access key
- Accelerator table
- Common User Access
- Computer keyboard
- Human interface guidelines
- Pointing device gesture
- StickyKeys
- Table of keyboard shortcuts

Notes and references

[1] In the English language a "shortcut" may unintentionally suggest an incomplete or sloppy way of completing something. Consequently, some computer applications designed to be controlled mainly by the keyboard, such as Emacs, use the alternate term "key binding".

[2] Lowensohn, Josh (3 December 2009). "Hardware for Gmail: The 'Gboard' keyboard" (http://news.cnet.com/8301-27076_3-10409035-248.html). CNET.com. . Retrieved 7 January 2011.

[3] "Using Accesskeys - Is it worth it?" (http://www.wats.ca/show.php?contentid=32). wats.ca. October 2006. . Retrieved 7 January 2011.

External links

- Large database of keyboard shortcuts (search by application, software category, operating system) (http://www.keyxl.com)
- mnemonic definition on SUN glossary (http://java.sun.com/products/jlf/ed2/book/HIG.Glossary.html#51661)
- Differences between keyboard shortcuts and mnemonics (http://blog.i18n.ro/keyboard-shortcuts-and-mnemonics-or-accelerators-are-not-the-same-thing/)
- Video Game Keyboard Charts (http://isometricland.com/keyboard/keyboard.php) - Small graphical database of video game keyboard bindings.

Health_(gaming)

Health is a game mechanic used in tabletop role-playing games and video games to give value to characters, enemies, NPCs, and related objects. This value can either be numerical, semi-numerical as in **hit/health points**, or arbitrary as in a **life bar**.

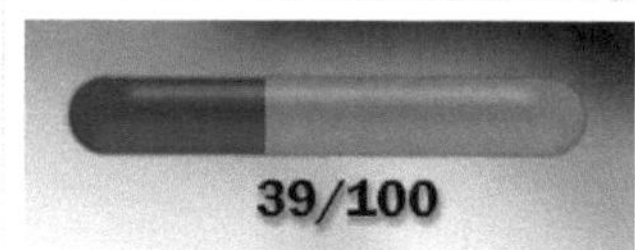

A 'life bar', a possible representation of the health of an object.

Hit points

Hit points, also known as health points (or HP), damage points, heart points, or just health (among other synonyms), is a finite value used to determine how much damage (usually in terms of physical injury) a character can withstand. When a character is attacked, or is hurt from a hazard or fall, the total damage dealt (which is also represented by a point value) is subtracted from their current HP. Once their HP reaches 0, the character will be unable to fight. In role-playing games, health is often abbreviated by two letter initialisms such as HP.

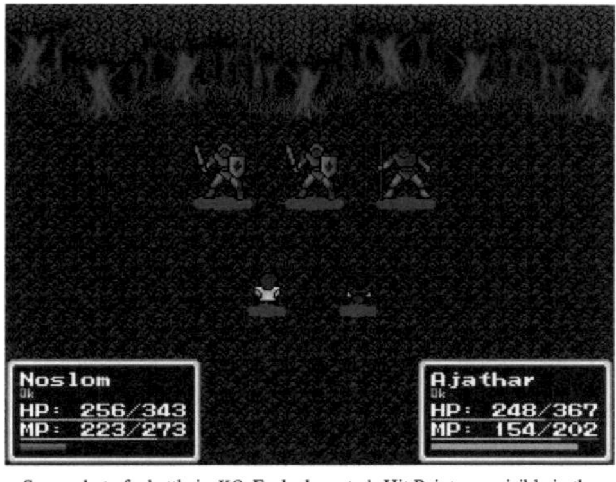

Screenshot of a battle in *KQ*. Each character's Hit Points are visible in the corner boxes, and the white filling on the bar indicates the percentage of the character's health that remains.

In some role-playing games such as *Dungeons & Dragons*, a player character's hit points are determined by character level. The hit points of monsters are decided by rolling "Hit Dice". Characters with high constitution will have an advantage when hit points are assigned. A character whose hit points are reduced to zero is considered dead or incapacitated. Other games sometimes lack levels, hit points, or both.

In certain editions of the game, player characters with 0 HP are not dead, but rather knocked unconscious. Within the range of -1 and -9, they are considered to be mortally wounded and dying, and their HP will steadily drop until it is stabilized. At -10, the character dies. Depending on the rules, a character who suffers 50+ points of damage from a single blow may die as a result of "Death from Massive Damage".[1] The player must then make a "saving throw" of the dice in hope of countering the damage. Failure to do so results in the characters dying, regardless of their remaining HP.

In many role-playing video games, the objective is to deplete the hit points of enemies while maintaining the health of player characters. Hit points can typically be refilled by using a restorative item, staying the night at an "inn", or utilizing healing magic. Generally, characters are killed or rendered unconscious as soon as their hit points reach 0.

History

Dungeons & Dragons co-creator David Arneson described the origin of hit points in a 2002 interview. When Arneson was adapting the medieval wargame *Chainmail* to a fantasy setting, a process that with Gary Gygax would lead to the game *Dungeons & Dragons*, he saw that the emphasis of the gameplay was moving from large armies to small groups of heroes and eventually to the identification of one player and one character that is so essential to role-playing as it was originally conceived. Players became attached to their heroes and did not want them to die every time they lost a die roll. Players were given multiple hit points which were then incrementally decreased. Arneson took the concept, along with armor class, from a set of a naval American Civil War game's rules.[2]

Life bar

A *health* or *life bar* is used to display a character's health in many video games. A typical life bar is a horizontal rectangle which begins full of color. If damage is taken or mistakes are made, the colored area gradually reduces (some also change colour, typically from green to yellow to red, as health is reduced). When the bar is completely emptied, the result is game over (death, being knocked out, etc.). In 1984, both the arcade game *Dragon Buster* and computer game *Gemstone Warrior* first used a bar to represent "health".[3] There have since been many variations on the life bar:

In *Street Fighter* and other fighting games, the bar does not instantly immediately decrease when damage is taken. Instead, an area representing the damage is marked in red, and the health lost quickly drains away. This is useful in assessing the amount of damage caused by an attack.

Some games use an incremental bar, composed of many smaller bars. Each attack will remove a certain number of these bars. This system is used in the *Mega Man* series.[4]

Some video games also feature a recharging health bar. In these games, the player character cannot usually take as much damage as a player with a traditional life bar, but health regenerates over time (usually initiating regeneration when the player avoids being damaged for a period of time). Notable examples of this are the *Hydlide* series, *Ys* series,[5] [6] *Halo* series, *Call of Duty* series, *Destroy All Humans!*, *Gears of War*, *Tom Clancy's Rainbow Six Vegas*, *Tom Clancy's Splinter Cell Double Agent*, and *Red Steel*. Some games may increase the maximum health limit of the player character as they progress through the game.

Icon-based health

Heart-shaped icons can indicate the amount of health a player has left.

Icons are another method for measuring health. Some games such as *Prince of Persia*, *DuckTales*, and *Mr. Nutz*, which use a number of icons to represent health units; every hit against the player character will always decrease health by one icon or unit at a time. In other games a hit may reduce health by one icon or unit, a fraction of one icon, or many icons at once, depending on how powerful the hit is, and the strength of the character's defence of armour. In most of the games in the *The Legend of Zelda* series of video games, the player's health is represented as small hearts.[4] Weak attacks against the player will take only a fraction of a heart, usually one-quarter or one-half, and stronger attacks may take many whole hearts at once. Several games make use of similar heads-up displays. *Super Mario Bros. 2* uses small red icons (in 16-bit versions of the game, they're changed to hearts) in the top left corner to designate how many hitpoints the player has remaining, and *Bram Stoker's Dracula* uses small flasks of liquid. The game Minecraft uses Hearts to display Health, like Legend of Zelda, but damage will not reduce quarters of a heart, rather, the minimum is half a Heart, but attacks can drain multiple hearts, depending on damage and player's armor.

Other games, such as *Deus Ex*, show a HUD of a human body, which is green to begin with. As the player takes damage, the respective region of the body turns yellow, orange, red, and eventually disappears altogether. For the head and torso, this is fatal. For arms, this causes a significant decrease in weapon accuracy or damage (or a complete inability to use them), while such a damage for legs usually leads to a badly impaired movement. A similar system, but showing the player's current vehicle rather than a human body, is used in some simulation games such as *Rogue Squadron*.

Other variations

Recharging health

Some games use a system of *recharging* health (or regeneration), where health points are regained over a short period of time (usually minutes). This mechanic has its origins in Roguelike games of the 1980s. In the 2000s, the mechanic was popularized among first-person shooters by the *Halo* series, while action RPGs such as *Fable* have continued to utilize the mechanic.

Other games require the use of healing spells, skills, or items (such as potions, medicine, first aid kits, bandages, syringes, medical bags, herbs, and even food) to regain health. Many game systems incorporate both slow regeneration and instant-effect healing skills and items. Games often have items that recharge all or some of a character's health, but they may differ in that, some games allow the player character to collect and carry many items in an inventory and use them to recharge health at a later time when needed; while in other games the player character cannot carry items in such a way and items will recharge health immediately upon touching them or sometimes upon picking them up. If such health recharching items are carried, the player usually needs to manually select the item and use it before their health completely runs out. Some games however contain items that, when carried, automatically revive a character when their health reaches zero and restores them to either full or part health.

Another common way of repleneshing health in games is to have a number of fixed locations that characters can travel to, and where their health will be replenished either for free, or by paying some in game currency. These facilities can usually be used an unlimited number of times, and themes such as resting at an inn or character's home or base, drinking from a fountain, visiting a hospital or other medical facility, or visiting a person or location that heals with magic have all been used across different games and genres.

An increasingly common standard, is a complete lack of any health-replenishing items—the wounded player is simply expected not to take damage by taking cover and wait (generally from 5–20 seconds) as his or her character recovers. Most of these games do not feature a health meter; the player judges his or her health from blood on the screen, heavy breathing, and other details.

Incremental health

In the *Sonic the Hedgehog* series, the player character collects rings, which are usually used as his or her health indicator. They are shown as numbers at the upper left side of the screen. Whenever the player character takes damage when he or she does not have a shield, all of the player's rings scatter in many directions. If the player is fast enough, the player can reclaim some of the rings before they flicker and disappear. However, if the player character possesses a shield and takes a hit that the shield is not invulnerable against, the shield is lost and the player character will keep all of his or her rings. Almost all of the player characters can be killed instantly if they do not possess any rings or a shield when they take any damage. Sonic's rings differ from most health mechanisms in that having multiple rings offers no extra protection; however many rings a player possesses, all will be lost with one hit. However, some newer Sonic games such as *Sonic Blast*, *Sonic the Hedgehog*, *Sonic and the Secret Rings*, *Shadow the Hedgehog* and *Sonic Unleashed* have attempted to increase the fairness of this system by having the player lose only a set number of rings per hit (usually ten or twenty), meaning that having more rings provides better protection.

Percentage meter

In the *Super Smash Bros.* series, instead of health bars featured in most fighting games, percentage meters are used. When attacking an opponent or being attacked by an opponent, the percentage meter rises based on the damage inflicted; as the percentage meter increases, the character gradually becomes easier to knock away with strong attacks, possibly getting knocked out of the arena and, thus, losing either a life or a point, depending on the mode of play. In the Stamina mode, health percentage is used. When the character falls off of the stage, they are disqualified from the battle.

Health represented without Heads-Up Display

In order to immerse the player in the gaming experience, some developers do away with the health bar (and other on-screen displays) completely and try to present a character's health in other ways, such as showing a character limping or displaying visible wounds when they are injured. *Jurassic Park: Trespasser* (1998) has no HUD and represents its player character's (Anne) health as a heart-shaped tattoo on her breast which fills up with red as the damage increases. When she dies, the heart has a chain around it. In the early *Resident Evil* (1996–present) video games, health is shown both with the player character limping and pressing his/her wounds in pain, and with an EKG display in the inventory screen. Games such as *Call of Duty 2* (2005) or *Peter Jackson's King Kong: The Official Game of the Movie* (2005) have no life bar; instead, the game uses the screen as health, and when the player gets hit, the screen flashes red, and in some games the vision will also becomes blurred in this condition (more damage indicated by a deeper red coloration). In some games, characters slouch over and breathe heavily as a result of low health when left idle; blood stains or wounds may also appear on characters to show they are injured. Some third-person games such as *Dead Space* (2008) and *Ghostbusters: The Video Game* (2009) have health bars shown on the player model rather than in a HUD. They resemble ordinary health meters apart from being physically attached to the character's equipment.

See also

- Experience point
- Heads-up display
- Magic points

References

[1] Massive Damage Threshold and Results (http://www.d20srd.org/srd/variant/adventuring/massaveDamageThresholdsAndResults.htm). The Hypertext d20 SRD (http://www.d20srd.org/index.htm). Retrieved on 2008-3-24.

[2] Allen Rausch. "Dave Arneson Interview." (http://pc.gamespy.com/articles/540/540395p1.html). GameSpy. 2004-08-19. . Retrieved on 2008-3-24.

[3] "Gaming's most important evolutions" (http://www.gamesradar.com/f/gamings-most-important-evolutions/a-20101008102331322035/p-4). GamesRadar. Oct 8, 2010. p. 4. . Retrieved 2011-03-29.

[4] Chris Antista. "The 10 most creative life bars. (page 2)" (http://www.gamesradar.com/f/the-10-most-creative-life-bars/a-20100818124023804099/p-2). GamesRadar. 2010-08-17. . Retrieved on 2010-8-19.

[5] Szczepaniak, John (7 July 2011). "Falcom: Legacy of Ys" (http://imageshack.us/f/32/yshistory02.jpg/). *Games™* (111): 152–159 [153]. . Retrieved 2011-09-07. (cf. Szczepaniak, John (July 8, 2011). "History of Ys interviews" (http://blog.hardcoregaming101.net/2011/07/history-of-ys-interviews-by-john.html). *Hardcore Gaming 101*. . Retrieved 6 September 2011.)

[6] Kurt Kalata & Robert Greene. "Hydlide" (http://www.hardcoregaming101.net/hydlide/hydlide.htm). Hardcore Gaming 101. . Retrieved 2011-05-01.

Graphics_software

In computer graphics, **graphics software** or **image editing software** is a program or collection of programs that enable a person to manipulate visual images on a computer.

A screenshot from the vector graphics editor Inkscape

Computer graphics can be classified into two distinct categories: raster graphics and vector graphics. Many graphics programs focus exclusively on either vector or raster graphics, but there are a few that combine them in interesting ways. It is simple to convert from vector graphics to raster graphics, but going the other way is harder. Some software attempts to do this.

In addition to static graphics, there are animation and video editing software.

Most graphics programs have the ability to import and export one or more graphics file formats.

The use of a swatch is a palette of active colours that are selected and rearranged by the preference of the user. A swatch may be used in a program or be part of the universal palette on an operating system, it is used to change the colour of a project, that may be text, image or video editing. Vector graphics animation can be described as a series of mathematical transformations that are applied in sequence to one or more shapes in a scene. Raster graphics animation works in a similar fashion to film-based animation, where a series of still images produces the illusion of continuous movement.

History

SuperPaint (1973) was one of the earliest graphics software applications.

Fauve Matisse (later Macromedia xRes) was a pioneering program of the early 1990s, notably introducing layers in customer software.[1]

Currently Adobe Photoshop is one of the most used and best-known graphics programs, having displaced more custom hardware solutions in the early 1990s, but was initially subject to various litigation. GIMP is a popular open source alternative to Adobe Photoshop.

Other applications include:

- JPhotoBrush Pro, Java-based multi-platform, freeware.[2]
- Corel Paint Shop Pro

See also

- Comparison of raster graphics editors
- Comparison of vector graphics editors
- Graphics hardware
- List of raster graphics editors
- List of vector graphics editors
- Graphic art software
- Image conversion
- Photoshop
- Raster graphics editor
- Vector graphics editor

References

[1] Macromedia Matisse (http://pages.swcp.com/rtoads/vivisect/software/matisse.html), Reign of Toads (http://pages.swcp.com/rtoads/)
[2] JPhotoBrush Pro (http://www.jphotobrushpro.com)

Color_space

A color model is an abstract mathematical model describing the way colors can be represented as tuples of numbers, typically as three or four values or *color components* (e.g. RGB and CMYK are color models). However, a color model with no associated mapping function to an absolute color space is a more or less arbitrary color system with no connection to any globally understood system of color interpretation.

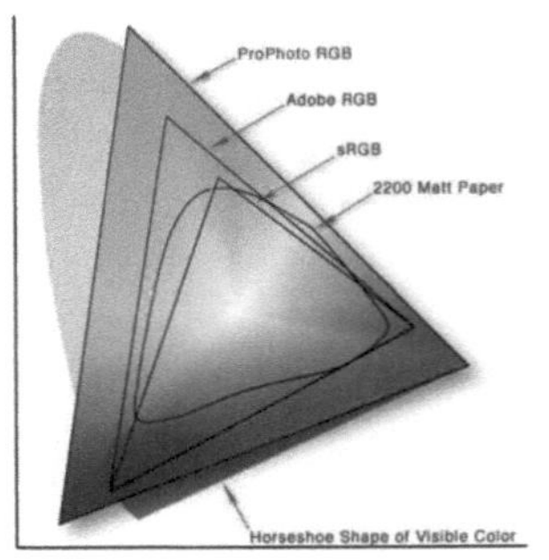

A comparison of the chromaticities enclosed by some color spaces.

Adding a certain mapping function between the color model and a certain reference color space results in a definite "footprint" within the reference color space. This "footprint" is known as a gamut, and, in combination with the color model, defines a new **color space**. For example, Adobe RGB and sRGB are two different absolute color spaces, both based on the RGB model.

In the most generic sense of the definition above, color spaces can be defined without the use of a color model. These spaces, such as Pantone, are in effect a given set of names or numbers which are defined by the existence of a corresponding set of physical color swatches. This article focuses on the mathematical model concept.

Understanding the concept

A wide range of colors can be created by the primary colors of pigment (cyan (C), magenta (M), yellow (Y), and black (K)). Those colors then define a specific color space. To create a three-dimensional representation of a color space, we can assign the amount of magenta color to the representation's X axis, the amount of cyan to its Y axis, and the amount of yellow to its Z axis. The resulting 3-D space provides a unique position for every possible color that can be created by combining those three pigments.

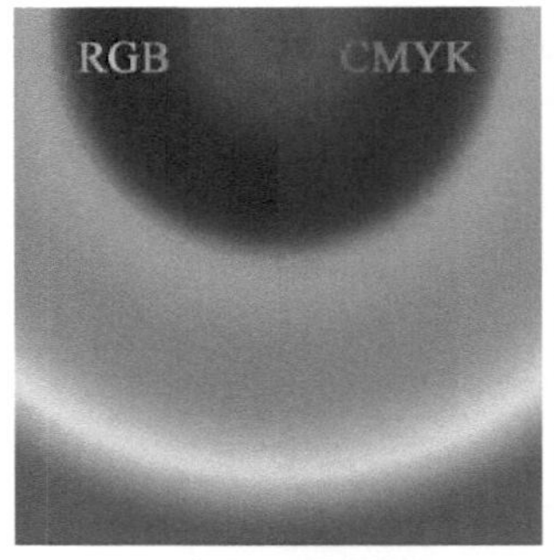

A comparison of RGB and CMYK color models. This image demonstrates the difference between how colors will look on a computer monitor (RGB) compared to how they will reproduce in a CMYK print process.

However, this is not the only possible color space. For instance, when colors are displayed on a computer monitor, they are usually defined in the RGB (red, green and blue) color space. This is another way of making nearly the same colors (limited by the reproduction medium, such as the phosphor (CRT) or filters and backlight (LCD)), and red, green and blue can be considered as the X, Y and Z axes. Another way of making the same colors is to use their Hue (X axis), their Saturation (Y axis), and their brightness Value (Z axis). This is called the HSV color space. Many color spaces can be represented as three-dimensional (X,Y,Z) values in this manner, but some have more, or fewer dimensions, and some, such as Pantone, cannot be represented in this way at all.

Notes

When formally defining a color space, the usual reference standard is the CIELAB or CIEXYZ color spaces, which were specifically designed to encompass all colors the average human can see.

Since "color space" is a more specific term for a certain *combination* of a color model plus a mapping function, the term "color space" tends to be used to also identify color models, since identifying a color space automatically identifies the associated color model. Informally, the two terms are often used interchangeably, though this is strictly incorrect. For example, although several specific color spaces are based on the RGB model, there is no such thing as *the* RGB color space.

Since any color space defines colors as a function of the absolute reference frame, color spaces, along with device profiling, allow reproducible representations of color, in both analogue and digital representations.

Conversion

Color space conversion is the translation of the representation of a color from one basis to another. This typically occurs in the context of converting an image that is represented in one color space to another color space, the goal being to make the translated image look as similar as possible to the original.

Density

The RGB color model is implemented in different ways, depending on the capabilities of the system used. By far the most common general-used incarnation as of 2006 is the 24-bit implementation, with 8 bits, or 256 discrete levels of color per channel. Any color space based on such a 24-bit RGB model is thus limited to a range of 256×256×256 ≈ 16.7 million colors. Some implementations use 16 bits per component for 48 bits total, resulting in the same gamut with a larger number of distinct colors. This is especially important when working with wide-gamut color spaces (where most of the more common colors are located relatively close together), or when a large number of digital filtering algorithms are used consecutively. The same principle applies for any color space based on the same color model, but implemented in different bit depths.

Partial list of color spaces

CIE 1931 XYZ color space was one of the first attempts to produce a color space based on measurements of human color perception (earlier efforts were by James Clerk Maxwell, König & Dieterici, and Abney at Imperial College)[1] and it is the basis for almost all other color spaces. Derivatives of the CIE XYZ space include CIELUV, CIEUVW, and CIELAB.

Generic color models

RGB uses additive color mixing, because it describes what kind of *light* needs to be *emitted* to produce a given color. Light is added together to create form from out of the darkness. RGB stores individual values for red, green and blue. RGBA is RGB with an additional channel, alpha, to indicate transparency.

Common color spaces based on the RGB model include sRGB, Adobe RGB and ProPhoto RGB.

CMYK uses subtractive color mixing used in the printing process, because it describes what kind of inks need to be applied so the light *reflected* from the substrate and through the inks produces a given color. One starts with a white substrate (canvas, page, etc.), and uses ink to subtract color from white to create an image. CMYK stores ink values for cyan, magenta, yellow and black. There are many CMYK color spaces for different sets of inks, substrates, and press characteristics (which change the dot gain or transfer function for each ink and thus change the appearance).

Additive color mixing: Three overlapping lightbulbs in a vacuum, adding together to create white.

YIQ was formerly used in NTSC (North America, Japan and elsewhere) television broadcasts for historical reasons. This system stores a luminance value with two chrominance values, corresponding approximately to the amounts of blue and red in the color. It is similar to the YUV scheme used in most video capture systems[2] and in PAL (Australia, Europe, except France, which uses SECAM) television, except that the YIQ color space is rotated 33° with respect to the YUV color space. The YDbDr scheme used by SECAM television is rotated in another way.

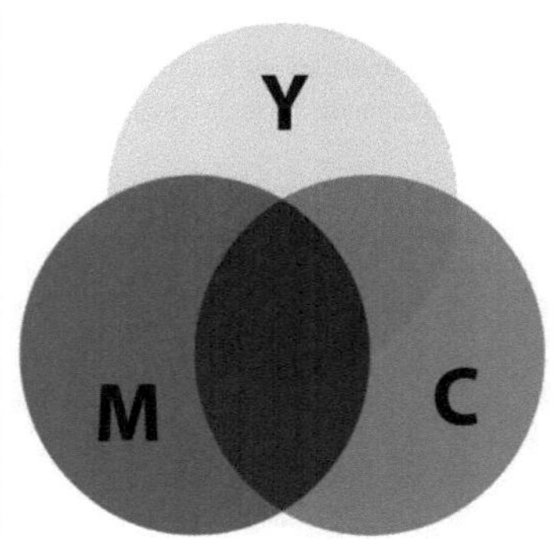

Subtractive color mixing: Three splotches of paint on white paper, subtracting together to turn the paper black.

YPbPr is a scaled version of YUV. It is most commonly seen in its digital form, YCbCr, used widely in video and image compression schemes such as MPEG and JPEG.

xvYCC is a new international digital video color space standard published by the IEC (IEC 61966-2-4). It is based on the ITU BT.601 and BT.709 standards but extends the gamut beyond the R/G/B primaries specified in those standards.

HSV (**h**ue, **s**aturation, **v**alue), also known as HSB (hue, saturation, **b**rightness) is often used by artists because it is often more natural to think about a color in terms of hue and saturation than in terms of additive or subtractive color components. HSV is a transformation of an RGB colorspace, and its components and colorimetry are relative to the RGB colorspace from which it was derived.

HSL (**h**ue, **s**aturation, **l**ightness/**l**uminance), also known as HLS or HSI (hue, saturation, **i**ntensity) is quite similar to HSV, with "lightness" replacing "brightness". The difference is that the *brightness* of a pure color is equal to the brightness of white, while the *lightness* of a pure color is equal to the lightness of a medium gray.

Commercial color spaces

- Munsell color system
- Natural Color System (NCS)

Special-purpose color spaces

- The RG Chromaticity space is used in Computer vision applications. It shows the color of light (red, yellow, green etc.), but not its intensity (dark, bright).

Obsolete color spaces

Early color spaces had two components. They largely ignored blue light because the added complexity of a 3-component process provided only a marginal increase in fidelity when compared to the jump from monochrome to 2-component color.

- RG for early Technicolor film
- RGK for early color printing

See also

- Color theory
- List of colors

References

[1] William David Wright, *50 years of the 1931 CIE Standard Observer*. Die Farbe, **29**:4/6 (1981).

[2] Dean Anderson. "Color Spaces in Frame Grabbers: RGB vs. YUV" (http://www.sensoray.com/support/frame_grabber_capture_modes.htm). . Retrieved 2008-04-08.

External links

- Color FAQ (http://www.poynton.com/ColorFAQ.html), Charles Poynton
- FAQ about color physics (http://www.colourware.co.uk/cpfaq.htm), Stephen Westland
- Color Science (http://www.physics.sfasu.edu/astro/color.html), Dan Bruton
- Color Spaces (http://www4.ncsu.edu/~rgkuehni/PDFs/ColSp.pdf), Rolf G. Kuehni (October 2003)
- Colour spaces - perceptual, historical and applicational background (http://ldos.fe.uni-lj.si/docs/documents/20030929092037_markot.pdf), Marko Tkalčič (2003)
- Color formats (http://www.equasys.de/colorformat.html) for image and video processing - Color conversion (http://www.equasys.de/colorconversion.html) between RGB, YUV, YCbCr and YPbPr.
- C library (http://pixfc-sse.googlecode.com) of SSE-optimised color format conversions.
- Konica Minolta Sensing: Precise Color Communication (http://www2.konicaminolta.eu/eu/Measuring/pcc/en/index.html)

Caps_lock

Caps lock is a key on many computer keyboards. Pressing it sets an input mode in which typed letters are uppercase by default (i.e. in All caps). The keyboard remains in caps lock mode until the key is pressed again. On some computers, holding down the shift key while caps lock is on temporarily switches to lowercase.

The caps lock key on a modern PC keyboard (near upper-left corner, below the Tab key)

User interfaces

Keyboards often include a small LED to indicate that caps lock is active—either on the key itself, or in a row with scroll lock and num lock indicators. However, some new laptop and wireless desktop keyboards lack the LED, instead providing software that gives an on-screen indicator.

Caps lock on an Apple Wireless keyboard. The green LED on the key is lit, indicating that caps lock is on.

People typing case-sensitive passwords that are not displayed verbatim on the screen may not realize that caps lock is on, causing errors. Help guides, tech support materials, and sometimes the interface itself may include advice on checking caps lock before typing a password. In Windows login screens, a warning that caps lock is on is shown in a balloon near the field. In Mac OS X, when caps lock is on, a caps lock symbol () is displayed inside a password field. Operating systems may also provide audible notifications when caps-lock, num-lock, or scroll-lock buttons are toggled.

Some manufacturers include an option in the controller software to deactivate the caps lock key. This behaviour allows users to decide themselves whether they want to use the key, or to disable it to prevent accidental activation.

History

The caps lock key is a modified version of the **shift lock** key that occupies the same position on the keyboards of mechanical typewriters. An early innovation in mechanical typewriters was the introduction of a second character on each typebar, thereby doubling the number of characters that could be typed, using the same number of keys. The second character was positioned above the first on the face of each typebar, and the shift key caused the entire type apparatus to move, physically *shifting* the positioning of the typebars relative to the ink ribbon. Just as in modern computer keyboards, the shifted position was used to produce capitals and secondary characters.

Because the shift key mechanism on a mechanical typewriter requires more force to operate and is usually operated by the little finger on the left hand, it was difficult to hold the shift down for more than two or three consecutive strokes. The shift lock key was introduced so the shift operation could be maintained indefinitely without continuous effort. It literally locked the shift mechanism, causing the upper character to be typed upon pressing any key.

The caps lock key on modern QWERTY keyboards differs from the shift lock key in that it capitalizes letters but does not affect other keys, such as numbers or punctuation. Some early computer keyboards, such as the Commodore 64, had a shift lock but no caps lock; others, such as the BBC Micro, had both, only one of which could be enabled at a time.

A version of caps lock that behaves like a traditional shift lock does exist on certain layouts such as the French AZERTY. Some operating systems and window managers allow caps lock to be used for a similar function. This behavior of the caps lock survives, however, in German and Austrian keyboards.

The keyboards of many early computer terminals, including the Teletype Model 33 ASR and Lear-Siegler ADM-3A, and early models of the IBM PC, positioned the Ctrl key where caps lock resides on modern keyboards.

The undesirable attributes of caps lock have led some power users to swap the positions of the two keys using aftermarket modifications; in the same vein, the One Laptop Per Child computers opt to place Ctrl in the caps lock position and discard caps lock entirely.[1] In a similar vein, the Google Cr-48 netbook replaces caps lock with a dedicated "Search" key.[2]

International Caps Lock Day

28 June and 22 October are annually marked as International Caps Lock Days as a parody holiday first noted in 2000.[3] [4] Rivaling Caps Lock Days have been since set up, such as 22 August.[5]

References

[1] Don Marti (2006-10-27). "Doing it for the kids, man: Children's laptop inspires open source projects" (http://www.linuxworld.com/news/2006/102706-childrens-laptops.html?page=3). Linux World. . Retrieved 2010-06-11.

[2] Diaz, Jesus (December 7, 2010). "Google wants to take your Caps Lock key away" (http://gizmodo.com/5708638/). Gizmodo. . Retrieved December 9, 2010.

[3] Brian, Matt (October 22, 2010). "Today is INTERNATIONAL CAPS LOCK DAY, but what is it?" (http://thenextweb.com/socialmedia/2010/10/22/today-is-international-caps-lock-day-but-what-is-it/). . Retrieved October 22, 2010.

[4] Blass, Evan (October 22, 2006). "HAPPY INTERNATIONAL CAPS LOCK DAY" (http://www.engadget.com/2006/10/22/happy-international-caps-lock-day/). The Next Web. . Retrieved October 22, 2010.

[5] "August Caps Lock Day" (http://www.facebook.com/event.php?eid=242361045781925). August 22, 2011. . Retrieved August 22, 2011.

External links

- Wiki:CapsLockOff—describes how to remap the caps lock key for other purposes.
- CAPSoff Official Website (http://capsoff.org/)
- Caps lock day official site. (http://capslockday.com/)

IBM PC keyboard (Windows, US layout)																				
Esc		F1	F2	F3	F4		F5	F6	F7	F8		F9	F10	F11	F12	PrtScn/ SysRq	ScrLk	Pause/ Break		

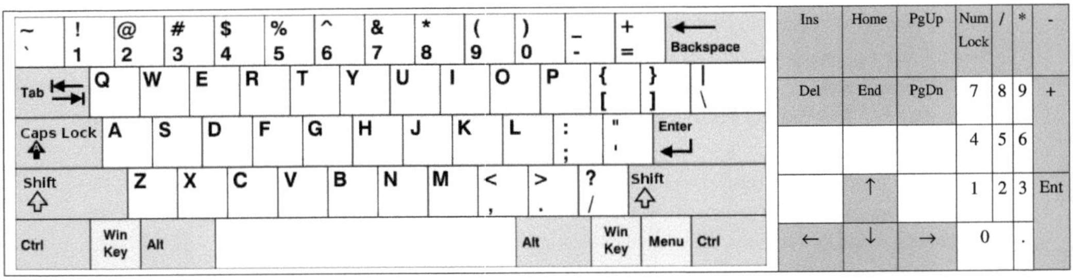

Scroll_lock

Scroll lock is an antiquated keyboard button (often with an associated status light) on some computer keyboards. The key is not needed or frequently used, and therefore some keyboards lack Scroll Lock altogether.[1]

The Scroll Lock key was meant to lock all scrolling techniques, and is a remnant from the original IBM PC keyboard, though it is not used by most modern-day software. In the original design, Scroll Lock was intended to modify the behavior of the arrow keys. When the Scroll Lock mode was on, the arrow keys would scroll the contents of a text window instead of moving the cursor. In this usage, Scroll Lock is a toggling lock key like Num Lock or Caps Lock, which have a state that persists after the key is released.

Today, this particular use of Scroll Lock is not used or rare. Only very few modern programs still honor this behavior, such as Lotus Notes, and Microsoft Excel. Most GUI environments neglect Scroll Lock, which means scrolling must be accomplished with a computer mouse, using means such as scrollbars or scroll wheels. Many common text editors (such as gedit, Notepad++, and Visual Studio) exhibit similar behaviour when arrow keys are used with control key depressed.

Pressing the Scroll Lock key in the Linux console while text is scrolling through the screen can freeze the application generating the output—during the duration of the freeze no further text accumulates in the buffer, but rather the output continues from where it left off after Scroll Lock is released. This allows the user to pause the display and read long messages that scroll through the screen too quickly to read, for example when the system is booting up (provided the keyboard driver has already been loaded).

Other uses

Because the key is otherwise rarely used, programs that tie into other software often use it to prevent issues arising from both programs using the same key. An example could be two game overlays using same shortcut, which will crash the game.

The indicator light is also sometimes used in certain applications,[2] as well as Keyboard Layout Indicator[3] [4] in some Linux distributions (like Ubuntu) because doing so is less likely to cause problems than manipulating other keys/lights.

In Microsoft Windows 2000 and later, a registry setting can be changed to enable a debugging feature that allows the user to manually crash the system, generating a memory dump for analysis. Once set, the user can hold the Ctrl key and tap the Scroll Lock key twice to trigger a BSOD.[5]

Belkin has released a 2-port KVM switch that uses the Scroll Lock key on the keyboard connected to the switch for selecting between computers. The switching is accomplished by pressing the Scroll Lock key twice, and then selecting either the "up" arrow key to select the first computer, or the "down" arrow key to select the second computer connected to the switch.

See also

- System request
- Pause/Break Key
- AltGr key

References

[1] "Keyboard - General Discussion" (http://forums.logitech.com/logitech/board/message?board.id=general&message.id=11846#M11846). Logitech. 2008-08-28. . Retrieved 26 November 2008. "this keyboard does not have a Scroll Lock key"

[2] "Illuminated Keyboard Hack" (http://www.instructables.com/id/Illuminated-Keyboard-Hack/). Kipkay(via Instructables). 2008-05-30. . Retrieved 25 July 2011. "Using the Scroll Lock key for illuminating your keyboard"

[3] 11.JPG (http://uc.exteenblog.com/padcharee/images/12/11.JPG) (การใช้งาน Ubuntu | SAMUTSAKHON FOUNDATION)

[4] Keyboard Layout Options, Keyboard Preferences (http://library.gnome.org/users/user-guide/2.32/prefs-keyboard.html.en#prefs-keyboard-layoutoptions) (Desktop User Guide - GNOME Library)

[5] "Windows feature lets you generate a memory dump file using the keyboard" (http://support.microsoft.com/kb/244139). Microsoft Corporation. . Retrieved 25 September 2011.

External links

- Straightdope article about the Scroll Lock key (http://www.straightdope.com/mailbag/mscrolllock.html)

IBM PC keyboard (Windows, US layout)

Esc		F1	F2	F3	F4		F5	F6	F7	F8		F9	F10	F11	F12	PrtScn/ SysRq	ScrLk	Pause/ Break				

~ `	! 1	@ 2	# 3	$ 4	% 5	^ 6	& 7	* 8	(9	) 0	_ -	+ =	Backspace	Ins	Home	PgUp	Num Lock	/	*	-
Tab	Q	W	E	R	T	Y	U	I	O	P	{ [	}]	| \	Del	End	PgDn	7	8	9	+
Caps Lock	A	S	D	F	G	H	J	K	L	: ;	" '	Enter					4	5	6	
Shift	Z	X	C	V	B	N	M	< ,	> .	? /	Shift				↑		1	2	3	Ent
Ctrl	Win Key	Alt		Alt	Win Key	Menu	Ctrl							←	↓	→	0		.	

Article Sources and Contributors

Status_bar *Source*: http://en.wikipedia.org/w/index.php?title=Status_bar *Contributors*: AVRS, Adam850, Boyton, Brenton, CesarB, Eva-psyche, Gaius Cornelius, Heptite, Hooperbloob, Marcus Qwertyus, Maxim, Minghong, Mjuarez, NYKevin, Niteling, Nonpareility, Omegatron, Rfc1394, Riba, Sardanaphalus, SebastianHelm, Simeon, Strait, Wikid77, Ynhockey, 25 anonymous edits

Window_(computing) *Source*: http://en.wikipedia.org/w/index.php?title=Window_%28computing%29 *Contributors*: 16@r, Ahunt, Aij, Al Lemos, AlistairMcMillan, Andy16666, Azrael Nightwalker, Baron1984, Baryonic Being, Benny476, BiT, BlueGuy213, Camilo Sanchez, CapitalR, Centrx, ChrisGualtieri, Cometstyles, Ctachme, DanielPharos, David Gerard, Detroit, Diego Moya, Dysprosia, EdC, Eduloqui, Fredrik, Gbleem, GermanX, Graham87, Gudeldar, JForget, Jerryobject, Jim10701, Jmabel, JoanneB, Joeblakesley, John Fader, KenanSulayman, Leevclarke, Lupin, Magioladitis, Marc Mongenet, Markblaster, Master2841, Megamanfan3, MichaelMcGuffin, Minghong, Morning277, Nigelj, Ojigiri, Omegatron, Patrick, PeepP, Peter S., Pnm, Pomte, Powerbutton, RadioFan, Rccarman, Rechtar, ReconTanto, Robofish, RockMFR, Rodeosmurf, Sanmartin, Sardanaphalus, Sayden, SebastianHelm, Sevenplusone, Sfoske70, Shadow demon, Sikon, SkyWalker, Smyth, Srtxg, Storkk, Suisui, Szhaider, Tarquin, Trevj, TuukkaH, Twp, Useight, Wafulz, Wapcaplet, Wraithdart, Zarcillo, Zeimusu, 84 anonymous edits

Graphical_user_interface *Source*: http://en.wikipedia.org/w/index.php?title=Graphical_user_interface *Contributors*: .:Ajvol:., 16@r, 3dguiman, A.t.bruland, ABF, ACupOfCoffee, Abrech, Accurastic, AeonicOmega, Aeternus, Ahoerstemeier, Akhristov, AlainV, Alan Liefting, Alan Millar, Alansohn, Alberto DV, Alexius08, Aliasd, Alisha.4m, AlistairMcMillan, Altenmann, Alvizal91, Am088, AmiDaniel, Amniarix, Anarchy103, Andreas Kaufmann, Andy16666, Andymc, Angelsfreeek, AnnaFrance, Anon2, Anonymous Cow, Anturiaethwr, Apl2007, Aric cramer, Ark, ArmadilloFromHell, Arnero, Arneth, Arthurrovich, Asdfwtf, AugustWind, Aviade, Axlq, B4hand, Badgernet, Barek, Barrera marquez, Basawala, Bdude, Belard, Bevo, Bgraabek, BiT, Blake-, Blanchardb, Bobnorwal, Bobo192, Bonaparte, Bongwarrior, Branddobbe, Brazucs, Brianreading, Bryan Derksen, Buddha24, Burgundavia, CWenger, Calabe1992, Caltas, CambridgeBayWeather, Can't sleep, clown will eat me, Carlo.Ierna, CattleGirl, Causa sui, Cerejota, Cfc123cfcxxx, Charivari, Charles Gaudette, Charlieleake, Chealer, Chirax, Chris 2010, Chrisch, Ciotog, Closedmouth, CommonsDelinker, Conversion script, CoolingGibbon, Corpx, Cuvtixo, Cyclonenim, DBigXray, DGG, DHN, DMAJohnson, DXBari, Dagibit, Damian Yerrick, Dancter, Daniel.Cardenas, Daniel5127, Darth Panda, David Gerard, David Shay, Davidhorman, Dbfirs, Delldot, DemeGeek, Denis C., DenisRS, Depot, Diannaa, Diego Moya, Djcraven, Dlohcierekim, DocWatson42, Doug Bell, Dpmuk, Dragice, Dragon 280, Dycedarg, EdC, Edcolins, Eddie tejeda, Edward, Ehurtley, El C, Epbr123, Eptin, Equalpants, Ewpoxy, ExplicitImplicity, FJPB, FT2, Falcon8765, Fang 23, Fastily, FatalError, FelixFT, Felixdakat, Fish and karate, FisherQueen, Fl, Flockmeal, Florianwardell, Fmccown, Forbsey, Frap, Frecklefoot, Freedom to share, Frozenport, Fsolda, G8orade, GRAHAMUK, Gaius Cornelius, Gary D, GeneMosher, Geniac, Gepwiki, Gerfaut, Gesslein, Ghettoblaster, Giftlite, GoingBatty, Gpearson2, Gpearson2isback, Graham87, GreenReaper, Grstain, Gumbos, Gwernol, Gzkn, Hadal, HairyPerry, HalfShadow, HamburgerRadio, Hapsiainen, HarisM, Haseo9999, Helpsloose, Heptite, Hexydes, Home-33bf7faecf., Hu12, Hut 8.5, Hutcher, Hydrogen Iodide, Hyung5kim, IanMAC, Icekiss, Ickyelf, Info@segger-us.com, Ivansanchez, J-stan, J.delanoy, JForget, JPaul, Jack O'Neill, Jackowaco, Jake7401, Jamesofur, JasonSADL, Jeffrey O. Gustafson, Jeffrey Smith, Jenny MacKinnon, Jerryobject, Jesse V., Jesus hands, Jfdwolff, JiMidnite, Jni, JoanneB, John Nowak, Jojit fb, Joshkaye0306, Jrousseau, Jtalledo, Juliancolton, Jwpurple, KDesk, KKong, Kaddds, Kasbjoernsen, Kbrose, KennyRogerz, Khalid hassani, Kim Bruning, Kinston eagle, KnowledgeOfSelf, Koman90, Krum Stanoev, Krystyn Dominik, Kulshrax, Kwamikagami, Kyle Barbour, Kyoko, Kızılsungur, LaggedOnUser, Lamro, Languagehat, Lanma726, Law, Le sacre, Lengoldberg, Lengyeltom, LeoNomis, Letdorf, Lightmouse, Linuxrules1337, Liontooth, LittleDan, Llamadog903, Lloydpick, LoganK, Longzheng, Loren.wilton, Lotje, M4gnum0n, MARKELLOS, MM23, Mac, Madmkh, MamaGeek, Mandarax, Manop, Manscher, Markpeak, Martarius, Massysett, Matjpow, Max Naylor, Max613, Mditto, Mdwh, Metal850, MichaelMcGuffin, Michelin106, Mig8tr, Mijter, Mike Rosoft, Mild Bill Hiccup, MilesTeg, Minesweeper, Minghong, Moa3333, ModusOperandi, Monty845, Mr Stephen, Mschel, Muhandes, Munchkinguy, Mushroom, Muslim Editor, Mwtoews, Mxn, NYKevin, Nanshu, Natkeeran, Naturalui, Navin Shetty Brahmavar, Nealmcb, Neodem, Nepalimora, Neurolysis, Nibuod, Night Gyr, Nixdorf, Nixeagle, Nohat, Nonagonal Spider, Northamerica1000, Nuclear Treason, Numbo3, Ohnoitsjamie, Oliver202, Omegatron, Oni Lukos, Onore Baka Sama, OrgasGirl, Ost316, PS2801, Palica, Pampas Cat, Paolo.dL, Paul August, Pegship, Phd holder, Philip Trueman, PhilipO, PhilippWeissenbacher, Piotrus, Polancox, Pooryorick, Postdlf, Premchai, PrimeCupEevee, Prunesqualer, Public Menace, Quietust, R r245, RadioFan, Raffaele Megabyte, RainbowOfLight, RajivManglani, RajivSBanga, Rajivmanglani, Rajnishbhatt, Ranhiru, RattleMan, Raven in Orbit, Rchandra, Reedy, RepublicanJacobite, Rettetast, Rfc1394, Rgoodermote, Rich Farmbrough, Richi, Rob Hooft, Robert Merkel, Ronhjones, Ronz, Rpawson, S.K., S32, SF007, Sam1234576, Samli1018, Samsview, Samtheboy, Sandius, Sango123, Sap123, Sardanaphalus, Scarykitty, Scisonic, Scott McNay, Sdmorgan, Sdornan, Seashorewiki, SebastianHelm, Sebthelodgemn, Seidenstud, Seigvaleheart, Semperf, Seth Nimbosa, Shadowjams, ShakingSpirit, Shamanchill, ShawnIsATard, Shizhao, Shoessss, Sintaku, SirGrant, Sjakkalle, Skyring, Slark, Sligocki, Slysplace, Smalljim, Somercet, Soumyasch, Sparkie82, SpeedyGonsales, Spike35031, Spitfire, Srinath1905, Starvinsky, StaticGull, Staxringold, Stephen B Streater, Stephen Hui, Stephenb, Stephenchou0722, Stonebluetree, StoryOfXentix, Stovetopcookies, StuffOfInterest, Super Rad!, Suso, Susvolans, Svick, System4200, Szajd, Tabletop, Tablizer, Takjji, TangentCube, Tangotango, Tannin, TarmoK, Tarquin, Tavilis, Tedickey, Tempshill, Teryx, Tghe-retford, TheSkinsFactory, Thedjatclubrock, TheresJamInTheHills, Thetorpedodog, Thomas Gilling, Thparkth, Tide rolls, TigerShark, Timlane, Tinsoul, Tizio, Tlesher, Tobias Hoevekamp, Todizzle91, Tomwhite56, Tornvmax, Trevj, Trusilver, Tubbimura91, Turnstep, Tuxcantfly, Twp, Ubuntude, Ucucha, Ukexpat, Unforgettableid, Uriash, Userdesign, Utcursch, Vaganyik, Vanished User 8a9b4725f8376, Vanished user 03, Vegfarandi, Veinor, ViperSnake151, Virtlink, Vivi6672, Vladsinger, VodkaJazz, VoluntarySlave, Vrenator, Vufors, W00FD0G, WJBscribe, WalterGR, Wapcaplet, Warren, Warut, Washburnmav, WatchAndObserve, Wavelength, Wendy.krieger, Wiki alf, Wiki13, Wikiloop, Wikivek, Willking1979, Woohookitty, WorldChampion392, Wrp103, WulfTheSaxon, Wvoutlaw2002, Ww, XJamRastafire, XgenZombie, Yamla, Youlovejoe, Zeeboid, ZeroOne, Zeus, דוד ש׳, ترجمان05, आशिष भटनागर, 934 anonymous edits

Web_browser *Source*: http://en.wikipedia.org/w/index.php?title=Web_browser *Contributors*: (, .Wiki.pedian., 16@r, 1712km, 216.15.88.xxx, 28421u2232nfenfcenc, 90 Auto, A-giau, ABF, ADeveria, AKMask, ARC Gritt, AceMyth, Adam Zivner, Adam78, Ade56facc, Ageekgal, Ahmad87, Ahoerstemeier, Airada, Akerbeltz, Akhristov, Aksn1p3r, Alan Liefting, Alan Millar, Alansohn, Alarchdu, Aldie, Alecmconroy, Aleenf1, AlefZet, Aleksa Lukic, Alessgrimal, Alevine-eantflick, AlistairMcMillan, Allstarecho, Althepal, AlumOxide, Amcfreely, Amg32009, Amog, An-chan, Andre Engels, Andres, Andrewferrier, Android79, Andy Marchbanks, Angr, Anna Lincoln, Antandrus, Anthony, Anthony Ivanoff, Antonio Lopez, Anypodetos, Anárion, Apswartz, Aquilosion, Aranea Mortem, Arcade, ArchStanton69, ArglebargleIV, Arkuat, Arvindn, Astroview120mm, Atenea26, AugPi, Auroranorth, Avoided, BadBoyMitch, Barek, Barneyboo, Beao, Beland, Ben-Zin, Benn08, Benregn, Bevo, BhuwanR, Bibliomaniac15, BigHairRef, BigSmoke, BirgerH, Bjankuloski06en, Blehfu, Blindgazer, Blue master24, BlueJ774, Bob bobato, Bobblehead, Bobo192, Bohemian Arcade, Bomac, Bonadea, Boomshadow, Boydbutler, Bozo33, Branddobbe, Branko, Brian Pearson, BruceB, Bubba hotep, Burgundavia, CWY2190, Cabalamat, Cacophony, Can't sleep, clown will eat me, CanadianLinuxUser, CanisRufus, CapitalSasha, Capricorn42, Captain panda, Carewolf, Carlj7, Carnildo, Carter, Caspertheghost, Celestianpower, Cerrigno, Charlesincharge, Chealer, Chicarelli, Chininazu12, Chinneeb, Chris55, Christian List, Chuck Marean, Chuck SMITH, ClamDip, Clasqm, Classicfilms, ClaudineChionh, Cloud 9, Clueless, CommonsDelinker, Conversion script, Copsi, Copysan, Crapizio, Crusadeonilliteracy, Cumuluscomputers, Curious1i, CyberSkull, Cyp, DARTH SIDIOUS 2, DamienRice, Daniel Hen, Daniel.Cardenas, DaughterofSun, DaveTheRed, DavidLevinson, De Surinamer, DeTru711, Dead3y3, Deekomalley, Den fjättrade ankan, Denisarona, Dephnit45, Derekland, Diamondjack2798, Digita, Digitalbyjess, Digitize, Discospinster, Dmickan, Dmsar, Doc glasgow, DocWatson42, Dowloadop, Dp76764, Dpsingh sac, DragonHawk, Dreamyshade, Drmies, Dysprosia, Eddyspeeder, Edmarriner, Eeekster, Ehheh, Ellmist, Eloquence, Elvey, Emperorbma, Emx, Eowend, Epbr123, Ericd, Espoo, Etz Haim, EugeneZelenko, Euryalus, Everyking, Evice, EvocativeIntrigue, Ewawer, Excirial, Explicit, Fabrictramp, Father Goose, Favonian, FedericoMP, Felipe Aira, Feydey, Ffaker, Fish and karate, Flarn2006, Fobenavi, FocalPoint, Fosnez, Frap, Fred Gandt, Fredrik, FrstFrs, Galorr, Galoubet, Gareth Aus, Gazpacho, Georgia guy, Ghettoblaster, Ghhgjjf, Giftlite, Glane23, Glenn, Gliese849b, Gogo Dodo, GoingBatty, GraemeL, Graham87, GreatWhiteNortherner, Greenrd, Grm wnr, Gsarwa, Gscshoyru, Gudeldar, Guliolopez, Guppy, HDCase, Hadal, Harp, Hbw, Hdk94, Headbomb, HeikoEvermann, Helix84, Henrik Gammelgaard, Hhielscher, HonorTheKing, Hoshie, Htaccess, Hymek, Iamjp180, Ilhanli, Imjustmatthew, Inferno, Lord of Penguins, Infogaufire, Ipodfanz, Irishguy, JFG, JMK, JOptionPane, JTBX, Jack No1, Jafeluv, Jahleeldaruis, Jaho, Jake Wartenberg, Jasper Deng, Javance, JayKeaton, Jebethe, Jeltz, Jerome2245, Jerryobject, Jerzy, Jesant13, JezWalters, Jezzabr, Jhsounds, Jinxed, Jleedev, Jmb kz, JoanneB, Joblio, John Fader, JonHarder, Jondel, Jor, JordanITP, Jordy577, Joshua Gyamfi, Joy, Joyous!, Jrtayloriv, Jtalledo, Jumpsports, Jusdafax, K2quill fairfax, Karen Johnson, Karl.brown, Katieh5584, Kazikameuk, Ke4roh, KelleyCook, Kevyn, Kgfleischmann, Kingpin13, Kku, Klingoncowboy4, KnowBuddy, KnowledgeOfSelf, Knutux, Kop, Kozuch, Kpjas, Krun, Kurowoofwoof111, Kuru, Kushalbiswas777, LGagnon, LaMenta3, Laurusnobilis, LeaveSleaves, Leuko, Lexter konsebio007, LeyteWolfer, LinguistAtLarge, Linuxerist, LittleDan, LittleMatchGirl, Livajo, Lotje, Louischengex 007, Lucyin, Lumpbucket, Lysdexia, Mabdul, Mac, Macwang, Marcus Qwertyus, Mark Renier, Matijap, MattieTK, Mattymcg, Mav, Meme xD, Mentaka, Metroryry, Metz2000, Michael Allan, MichaelBillington, Michaeljacksonfan, Midgrid, Miernik, Mikebrand, MikesPlant, Minesweeper, Minghong, Miquonranger03, MistaXFrye, Moe Epsilon, Mokgand, Monaarora84, Mormegil, Mortense, Motor, Mr. Bene, Mr. Lefty, Mr. Strong Bad, MrOllie, Mrschimpf, Mscwriter, Mulder416, Multifinder17, Mwarf, Mxn, Nakakapagpabagabag, Nanshu, Narsi90, Naudefj, Ncmvocalist, Nergaal, Neurodivergent, Niceguyedc, Nick, NickBush24, Nickshanks, Nietzsche 2, Nikai, Nikthestoned, Nintendo6110, Nixdorf, Noldoaran, Norm, Northstarweb, Nurg, Nyeguy, Oberiko, Ocaasi, Oicumayberight, Olmer, Oska, P0lyglut, PLJ, PM800, POOTER PIPER PIZZA, Papeschr, Patrick, Pcb21, Pegship, Persian Poet Gal, Peyre, Pgk, Philip Trueman, Piano non troppo, Pikiwyn, Pilaf, Pjoef, Plutonics, Pmsyyz, Poor Yorick, PranksterTurtle, Precious Roy, Precision Y, Premchakkungal, Primexx, Profoss, Public Menace, Puchiko, RSido, Rafaelluik, Randyoo, Ravensfan5252, RaviC, Rayis, RedRigel, Reedy, Reisio, Remember the dot, Repetition, Rhindle The Red, Richiekim, Rick Block, Roadwarrior52, Ronhjones, Rootbeer, Roy.vanegas, Rror, Rubber cat, Rugby471, RyanGerbil10, SB3606, SBKT, ST47, Sae1962, Sakurina, Salmar, Samboy, Samelliot01, Sampo Torgo, Sankalp.gautam, Schapel, Scodger4, Seajaywiki, Secretlondon, Seidenstud, Sevengen, Shalom Yechiel, Shenme, Siddsmat, Siliconglen, SilkTork, SimsimTee, Sincy55, Sinkhead101, Skizzik, Skyclown, Skysmith, Sl, Smalljim, Smyth, Sonjaaa, SpaceFlight89, Sparthorse, Speck-Made, Spitfire19, Splang, Squash, SqueakBox, Squids and Chips, Staeiou, StaticGull, Stephen Burnett, Stephenchou0722, Steve2011, SteveBaker, SteveSims, Steven Walling, Stickee, StopVandalsNow, Sumone10154, Superz3161981, Susfele, Svick, TGilmour, Tannin, TastyPoutine, Tawker, Tedickey, Terrycojones, Tgarsiel, That Guy, From That Show!, The Mysterious El Willstro, The Rambling Man, The RedBurn, The Thing That Should Not Be, The Wild Falcon, The bellman, The sock that should not be, TheParanoidOne, TheRingess, TheTechFan, Theaveng, Thecheesykid, Thedollelama, Theymos, Thorenn, Thumperward, Thurinym, Tide rolls, TimBentley, Tnxman307, Tobby72, Tomjenkins52, Tommy2010, Topleveldomainuser53, Towsonu2003, Tpbradbury, Traroth, Trasande, Trav1085, Trialsanderrors, Twibright Clock, UU, Ukexpat, Unknown W. Brackets, UnknownFork, Unslaked, Untermenschen, Unyoyega, Userafw, UsernameQQ, Vaganyik, Vancouverguy, Vary, Vbigdeli, Veinor, Versageek, Versus22, Vibhijain, Vishnava, WJetChao, WPjcm, WadeSimMiser, Waggers, Wallrunner51, Warren, Wavelength, Webbroser, Webera02, Wesley, Wfpoulet, Whkoh, Widefox, Wiifolderfan, Wikada, WikiED, WikiLeon, Wikifun95, Wikiolap, Wikiwiki, Wikiwikifast, Willking1979, Wimt, Wknight94, Wm, Wnissen, WojPob, Wolfehhgg, WorldlyWebster, Wtmitchell, WulfTheSaxon, Xdamr, Xiamcitizen, Xorx77, Yoctoinc, Yosri, Yukito-san, Zack, Zanimum, Zatorade, ZimZalaBim, Zollerriia, Zondor, Zoney, Zotterdas, Zundark, Александър, , 1032 anonymous edits

Text_mode *Source*: http://en.wikipedia.org/w/index.php?title=Text_mode *Contributors*: Ancheta Wis, AnonMoos, Canageek, Coolcaesar, DXBari, Damian Yerrick, Druiloor, Ed g2s, Fortdj33, Foxj, Frap, Funkymonkey, GreyCat, Incnis Mrsi, Kocio, Locador, Mahjongg, Marc Mongenet, Mindmatrix, Mjuarez, Monedula, Nczempin, NeonMerlin, Nihiltres, Pantergraph, Peter bertok, Qiuxing, R.123, Ricardo Cancho Niemietz, Richard W.M. Jones, Ricky81682, Sarrazip, Tedickey, Tobias Bergemann, Vendettax, Viznut, Wongm, Xe7al, ZeroOne, 21 anonymous edits

Keyboard_shortcut *Source*: http://en.wikipedia.org/w/index.php?title=Keyboard_shortcut *Contributors*: 149AFK, 16@r, 97198, @modi, A plague of rainbows, AMackenzie, Aapo Laitinen, Ace r91, Adrie7, Alansohn, Aleenf1, Alerante, Andylindsay, Anna Lincoln, Atoall, Axistive, BadmanMonkey, Bongwarrior, Brim, Caiaffa, Camerajohn, Catalim, Centrx, Chris the speller, CyberSkull, Cyberpower678, DXBari, Danorton, Deor, Dpirera, DragonHawk, Dreftymac, Excirial, Fayedizard, Fedallah, Feezo, Fiftyquid, Gadfium, GladiatorDisease, Howardyc, IOOI, Intersol, JForget, JTSchreiber, Jcamenisch, Jncraton, Joaopaulo1511, Jonathan Webley, Jowan2005, Joyous!, Kateshortforbob, Katieh5584, Kimero, Kiore, Kongr43gpen, Kvng, L337p4wn, Lee M, LeilaniLad, Loopy48, Mabdul, Marudubshinki, McLovin34, Michael Snow, MichaelMcGuffin, Mild Bill Hiccup, MisterHand, Mspraveen, Nikai, Niteling, Optakeover, Orbeverup, Osxshortcuts, Owlmonkey, Pantergraph, Petchboo, Piano non troppo, PigFlu Oink, PolarYukon, Ranmonster, Raul654, Rhopkins8, RobertG, Ronz, Salamurai, Scarian, Scientus, Scottperry, Shantu123, SharkD, Sijo Ripa, Softdevusa, Stentie, TPK, TheEgyptian, Thialfi, Thorenn, Tim R, TobyDZ, TravisMunson1993, Uncle G, Unfree, Useight, UtherSRG, Versageek, Vikrantkpr, Zwikipenguin, احمد مصطفى السيد, 128 anonymous edits

Health_(gaming) *Source*: http://en.wikipedia.org/w/index.php?title=Health_%28gaming%29 *Contributors*: AJComix, Annie E. Clarke, AspiringSquire, Athenai777, BlueAzure, Bobo192, Bomber332, Bridies, Carlwev, Cctoide, Chaheel Riens, Chaos5023, Chris Brehe, Darkwind, Eekerz, Elizium23, Face, Father Goose, Gary King, Haoma, Ibadibam, Imnotminkus, Inquam, Jagged 85, Jarble, Jeff Silvers, Jesse Viviano, Jgh913, JohnnyMrNinja, Johnnyfog, Joseph Solis in Australia, Jpark3909, Junevons, KLLvr283, Kintaro, Kitsunegami, Ksbrown, L Kensington, Luigifan, Marasama, Marasmusine, Master Deusoma, Message From Xenu, Misza13, NERVUN, Newk657, Nn123645, Northamerica1000, Oloddin, Ost316, Percy Snoodle, Popageorgio, QuagmireDog, RJaguar3, Radagast83, Sfan00 IMG, Sgeureka, SharkD, Slayerteez, Some guy, Someone another, SteinbDJ, Suzaku Medli, Teh Conscript, Tigernose, Tommy2010, TopGear, TowerDragon, Ultraexactzz, ViperSnake151, Xinator, Xomic, YVNP, ZicherCZ, Zzedar, אריה ה., 149 anonymous edits

Graphics_software *Source*: http://en.wikipedia.org/w/index.php?title=Graphics_software *Contributors*: .:Ajvol:., 16@r, Acidburn24m, Aldnonymous, Alex Ruddick, AySz88, Bashari, Biasoli, Clairesstone, Deineka, Donarreiskoffer, Eran of Arcadia, Fayenatic london, Freebieweb, Gerhardvalentin, Gonzonoir, IcedNut, Ijbond, Jacobolus, Jamelan, JonHarder, Kevin Whalen, Kranix, Leksey, Leon2323, Linuxerist, Lowellian, MBisanz, Marasmusine, Materialscientist, Maxí, Mercenario97, Mosca, NaBUru38, Nbarth, Oicumayberight, Oxymoron83, Peter Horn, Professoryak, RW Marloe, Radagast83, Remi de, ShaunMacPherson, Shawnc124, Skeleton771, Smalljim, Sole Soul, Someguy1221, TheParanoidOne, Thumperward, Vein eater, Versus22, Veyklevar, Vrenator, Walden, Wikipelli, Yerpo, 57 anonymous edits

Color_space *Source*: http://en.wikipedia.org/w/index.php?title=Color_space *Contributors*: 166.70.2.xxx, 28421u2232nfenfcenc, AUllrich, Aadnk, Aboalbiss, Aditsu, Adoniscik, AgentPeppermint, Alan Peakall, Alue, Arthena, Asc99c, Ashishbhatnagar72, Aubrey Jaffer, Aursani, Avsa, Beetstra, Benandorsqueaks, Bevo, Bobo192, BorgQueen, Branko, Brianski, Brona, CALR, CesarB, Chris the speller, Chrisc666, Chrumps, Colordoc, Conversion script, Cpesacreta, Cxw, Cy21, Cyp, Damian Yerrick, DariusMonsef, Darrien, Dave3457, David1217, Denelson83, Dkroll2, Dmurphy, Dominus, Dr.K., Dwandelt, FishSpeaker, Fredrik, Funandtrvl, Grendelkhan, Gutza, Hellisp, Heron, Hyacinth, ISteve, Jacobolus, Jay, Jhenderson777, Jim1138, Jonathan Webley, Josef Meixner, Kasper Hviid, Lambtron, Life of Riley, LittleDan, Lovibond, Marluxia.Kyoshu, Mfc, Mindmatrix, Misst r, Moeron, NekoDaemon, Neparis, Noldoaran, Normankoren, Notinasnaid, Odo1982, Orderud, PAR, Poccil, Rebornsoldier, Retired username, Rhebus, Rich Farmbrough, Richie, Rjwilmsi, Robartsd, Rythie, Sam Hocevar, SarahPalmerson, Sardanaphalus, Seabhcan, Seattlenow, SharkD, Skarebo, Sluzzelin, Smyth, SocratesJedi, Sparkit, Stephanej, Sterrys, Suruena, Sven271, Ta bu shi da yu, Tletnes, Twirligig, Uaxuctum, Umofomia, Wapcaplet, Zundark, 144 anonymous edits

Caps_lock *Source*: http://en.wikipedia.org/w/index.php?title=Caps_lock *Contributors*: 041744, 1000, 123456798, 5hin3, 7, A J Luxton, Acdx, Acroterion, Addshore, Al Lemos, Alagahd, Alansohn, Alerante, Alex Ji LT-21, Allens, Amikake3, Anakin101, AniRaptor2001, Anss123, Antilived, Apparition11, Aronk, Banaticus, Behn-kihl-nahm, BirdValiant, BodyTag, Bofur, Branddobbe, Brendangalligan, Brianga, Brucelee, Calsapidus, Canapple, Cantorman, Carbon-16, Caster23, ChaChaFut, Cheese cake 09, CheeseyPuff, CloudNine, Cmdrjameson, Colemak fan, Computer guy57, Courcelles, Crazycomputers, Cryptic, Cureden, Curps, Cybercobra, Dan100, DavidCary, Dbenbenn, Dcljr, DeadEyeArrow, Deathawk, Deliafcipe, Deliriousandlost, Dexter Nextnumber, Discospinster, Diti, Dmd, Dougofborg, Duncharris, Dweller, Dystopia9, EdGl, Eik Corell, Encephalon, Eraserhead1, Fences and windows, Filter1800, Fireplace, First Light, Fluffyhead55, Fosnez, Fran McCrory, FreplySpang, Fubar Obfusco, Gargaj, Ged UK, George2001hi, GoingBatty, GorillaWarfare, Gpvos, Gracenotes, Gradster1, Grey-Fox, Grinman, Gtg204y, Gudeiron, Guy Harris, HPeugeot, Havoc29, Haza-w, HanjaRoa, Hellknowz, Henkk78, HenriP, Herostratus, Highconclave, Iknowyourider, J.delanoy, JBsupreme, JJJJust, JamesBWatson, Jammycakes, Jbening, Jclemens, Jnelson09, Johngagon, Joshua Issac, Jpgordon, Jsnell, Jtle515, Juancnuno, JulianDelphiki, Jusdafax, Karl 334, Katieh5584, Kip36, Kueller1, LThomasUK, Lambtron, Lannacombe, Larry V, LarryMac, LeaveSleaves, LedgendGamer, Lenzar, Leon math, Lolqut, LordHedgie, Lordkatbert, Lysol, MER-C, MOHZAZMAD, Majorly, MartinRobinson, Maximaximax, Mechamind90, Meisterkoch, Mentifisto, Mernen, Message From Xenu, Micah hainline, Michaelas10, Millahnna, Momo56, Mpt, Mr. Wheely Guy, Mtcv, Myasuda, N-Man, Najoj, NawlinWiki, Nh.jg4, Nicgarner, Nmnogueira, OS2Warp, OneHitBlunder, Oni Ookami Alfador, Pampas Cat, Passionless, Patcat88, Paul August, Per Hedetun, Phobius, Piano non troppo, Plantpot2, Polyamorph, Pyritie, Pyro3000, QuantumEleven, RJaguar3, RVJ, Reach Out to the Truth, Rebent, Rlandmann, Rory096, Rudidude86, Russianmissile, Ryan4314, Saklhnp5288, Schaefer, SchuminWeb, Scootey, Scottbell, Sebleblanc, Silas S. Brown, Skyler72, Spufum, Steven Andrew Miller, Stevenrasnick, Swpb, Syrthiss, Tbhotch, Tealwisp, Teledildonix314, The Nixinator, TheDJ, TheKMan, TheKaneInformer, Thetux, Theymos, Thingg, ThomasMcPro, Three-Tail, Tide rolls, Tifego, Toddst1, Tommy2010, Totalporch2, Trendelltom, Trollfacelolol, Twinzor, Twooars, Vianello, Vicenarian, Vishahu, Vquex, Wa3frp, Wanderingstan, WereSpielChequers, Wikinist, Wqerty, Wysdom, Xenctuary, Yamamoto Ichiro, Zidane2k1, Zzuuzz, ♡, 389 anonymous edits

Scroll_lock *Source*: http://en.wikipedia.org/w/index.php?title=Scroll_lock *Contributors*: 041744, 203.109.250.xxx, 23pokrzywa, 24.4.254.xxx, 2D, AbderrahmanNajjar, Abelson, Academic Challenger, Ahoerstemeier, Alerante, Alereon, AlexanderM, Alphachimp, AnOddName, Anden21, Ann Stouter, Antandrus, Audioslave22, Bachrach44, Bavi H, Belegdal, Bigmacdaddy, Billgordon1099, Bobet, Bongwarrior, BorgHunter, Bped1985, Brian the Editor, Brian0918, BufferedIO, Burningnight, Byederek, CWenger, Calmer Waters, Chad Few, Chris Q, Chris the speller, Chuck Smith, Clickpop, Colonies Chris, CommunistHamster, Conversion script, Corpx, Cureden, Curlybap, DARTH SIDIOUS 2, DVdm, Da Vynci, Dan Guan, Dario D., Daserver, DaveTheRed, Dcljr, Deathtreath93, Discospinster, Disgracerpg, Dmerrill, Dom Kaos, Dpmuk, Draftplant0093, DragonflySixtyseven, Drummerman109, DuHxMaX, Edupedro, Elmer Clark, Enviroboy, Epbr123, Etzich, Exert, FleetCommand, Gab6894, Gardar Rurak, George The Dragon, Gertlex, Gilderien, Glenfarclas, Gorobay, Gracenotes, Graham87, Grue, Guliolopez, Hellspath, Helpsloose, Hibsch, Hiddekel, Hvjackson, IceKarma, Inkington, Insanity Incarnate, Inter, IntrigueBlue, Ishu991, J.delanoy, Jason Leach, Jay, Joehill11, JonHarder, Juliantwd, Kauczuk, Kwertii, Limulf, LindsayH, Lineslarge, Loelin, Lomn, LonelyBeacon, MKFM, Mappum, Marcovitaly, Marek69, Marshall Williams2, Martin-C, Matt Lib Soc, Mauls, Maxman280, Mditto, Mduser63, Michaelas10, Mrh30, Natl1, Naught101, Nburden, NeilFraser, Neoprogram, Nitro2k01, Northgrove, NoticeQuest, OcciMoron, Oni Lukos, PQuacrod, Pharaoh of the Wizards, Philip Trueman, Phnom Penh Punks, Possum, Przepla, Quanti, Qwfp, Ramaksoud2000, Redrocket, Remember the dot, Revolus, Rfc1394, Richard W.M. Jones, Roland Kaufmann, Ronark, Roxfan, SDWolf, SJP, Saayiit, SchmuckyTheCat, Scott14, SequoiaKangaroo, Sesu Prime, SheeEttin, Shoeofdeath, Sintaku, Slant, Some jerk on the Internet, Splintax, SqueakBox, Steven Zhang, Super-Magician, TJSwoboda, Tannin, TeaDrinker, Tech09, Texastoast78, Tgfcoder, The Epopt, The Thing That Should Not Be, The wub, The12game, TheAllSeeingEye, TheDJ, ThomasWinwood, Thumperward, Tiddly Tom, TigerK 69, TigerShark, Tim Starling, Timonczesq, Tjdw, Tobias Bergemann, Trivialist, Tslocum, Tuxlie, Twooars, Uhai, Ulric1313, Utsutsu, Viande hachée, Viriditas, WLU, WarthogDemon, Wik, Wilinckx, Wtmitchell, X-Fi6, Zalgo, Zerbey, Zeromaru, Zirka, 398 anonymous edits

Image Sources, Licenses and Contributors

File:Emacs statusline.png *Source*: http://en.wikipedia.org/w/index.php?title=File:Emacs_statusline.png *License*: unknown *Contributors*: Original uploader was Heptite at en.wikipedia

File:Gnome-2.16-screenshot.png *Source*: http://en.wikipedia.org/w/index.php?title=File:Gnome-2.16-screenshot.png *License*: unknown *Contributors*: Senori

File:Gimp-2.6.0.png *Source*: http://en.wikipedia.org/w/index.php?title=File:Gimp-2.6.0.png *License*: unknown *Contributors*: GOD ACRONYM at en.wikipedia

File:Expander.png *Source*: http://en.wikipedia.org/w/index.php?title=File:Expander.png *License*: unknown *Contributors*: EdC, original uploader at en.wikipedia

File:Windows 7.png *Source*: http://en.wikipedia.org/w/index.php?title=File:Windows_7.png *License*: unknown *Contributors*: Addihockey10, Althepal, AnOddName, Anakin101, Andyso, Anomie, AussieLegend, Bkell, Captaincollect1970, Crazlunatic, Drilnoth, Feinoha, FleetCommand, GSK, Grayshi, Jan Hofmann, JetBlast, Jjupiter100, Josh the Nerd, Koman90, LOL, LobStoR, Mephiles602, Ngyikp, Nicholas Love, OriginalGamer, PhilKnight, RegularBreaker, Roscelese, S0aasdf2sf, SF007, SchuminWeb, Sdrtirs, Seaphoto, Sonicdude558, Sotcr, SpaceFlight89, The 888th Avatar, Warren, Wtshymanski, 35 anonymous edits

File:Gnome 3.2 shell.png *Source*: http://en.wikipedia.org/w/index.php?title=File:Gnome_3.2_shell.png *License*: unknown *Contributors*: The GNOME Project

File:Xerox Alto.jpg *Source*: http://en.wikipedia.org/w/index.php?title=File:Xerox_Alto.jpg *License*: unknown *Contributors*: Barcex, Bayo, Clusternote, Daderot, Foofy, Grandy02, RedAndr

Image:X-Window-System.png *Source*: http://en.wikipedia.org/w/index.php?title=File:X-Window-System.png *License*: unknown *Contributors*: User:Liberal Classic

Image:Xerox 8010 compound document.jpg *Source*: http://en.wikipedia.org/w/index.php?title=File:Xerox_8010_compound_document.jpg *License*: unknown *Contributors*: Calmer Waters, Capricorn42, Diego Moya, Pointillist, Sfan00 IMG, 1 anonymous edits

Image:Bash screenshot.png *Source*: http://en.wikipedia.org/w/index.php?title=File:Bash_screenshot.png *License*: unknown *Contributors*: Akinom, Andrew pmk, Berland, Emx, Insuranze, Kahlil88, Leileilol, MarSoft, Pixel ;-), Shooke, Túrelio, 5 anonymous edits

File:Wikimedia browser share pie chart 3.png *Source*: http://en.wikipedia.org/w/index.php?title=File:Wikimedia_browser_share_pie_chart_3.png *License*: unknown *Contributors*: User:I384403

File:WorldWideWeb FSF GNU.png *Source*: http://en.wikipedia.org/w/index.php?title=File:WorldWideWeb_FSF_GNU.png *License*: unknown *Contributors*: Gürkan Sengün

File:Marc Andreessen.jpg *Source*: http://en.wikipedia.org/w/index.php?title=File:Marc_Andreessen.jpg *License*: unknown *Contributors*: Brian Solis

Image:Norton Utilities 6.01 UI.png *Source*: http://en.wikipedia.org/w/index.php?title=File:Norton_Utilities_6.01_UI.png *License*: unknown *Contributors*: Bilby, Ricardo Cancho Niemietz

Image:Character generator scheme.svg *Source*: http://en.wikipedia.org/w/index.php?title=File:Character_generator_scheme.svg *License*: unknown *Contributors*: User:Damian Yerrick, User:Incnis Mrsi

Image:Firefoxshortcuts.png *Source*: http://en.wikipedia.org/w/index.php?title=File:Firefoxshortcuts.png *License*: unknown *Contributors*: Petchboo, annotations by Intersol, Mozilla Foundation. Original uploader was Petchboo at en.wikipedia. Later version(s) were uploaded by Intersol at en.wikipedia.

File:Hitpoints.png *Source*: http://en.wikipedia.org/w/index.php?title=File:Hitpoints.png *License*: unknown *Contributors*: Decoy

File:KQ-hitpoints.png *Source*: http://en.wikipedia.org/w/index.php?title=File:KQ-hitpoints.png *License*: unknown *Contributors*: Chris Barry, Josh Bolduc, Rey Brujo, Eduardo Dudaskank, Master Goodbytes, Sam Hocevar, Peter Hull, Matthew Leverton, TeamTerradactyl, Troy D Patterson, Brandon Barnes, Rey Brujo, Günther Brammer, Edgar Alberto Molina

File:Lifebar-hearts.png *Source*: http://en.wikipedia.org/w/index.php?title=File:Lifebar-hearts.png *License*: unknown *Contributors*: User:RJaguar3

Image:Inkscape screenshot.png *Source*: http://en.wikipedia.org/w/index.php?title=File:Inkscape_screenshot.png *License*: unknown *Contributors*: Coyau, Damian Yerrick, Emc2, Fred J, Gliu, Mardus

Image:Colorspace.png *Source*: http://en.wikipedia.org/w/index.php?title=File:Colorspace.png *License*: unknown *Contributors*: Original uploader was Cpesacreta at en.wikipedia

File:RGB and CMYK comparison.png *Source*: http://en.wikipedia.org/w/index.php?title=File:RGB_and_CMYK_comparison.png *License*: unknown *Contributors*: User:Marluxia.Kyoshu

Image:AdditiveColor.svg *Source*: http://en.wikipedia.org/w/index.php?title=File:AdditiveColor.svg *License*: unknown *Contributors*: Original uploader was SharkD at en.wikipedia Later versions were uploaded by Jacobolus at en.wikipedia.

Image:SubtractiveColor.svg *Source*: http://en.wikipedia.org/w/index.php?title=File:SubtractiveColor.svg *License*: unknown *Contributors*: Original uploader was SharkD at en.wikipedia Later version uploaded by Jacobolus, Dacium at en.wikipedia.

Image:Keyboard-left keys.jpg *Source*: http://en.wikipedia.org/w/index.php?title=File:Keyboard-left_keys.jpg *License*: unknown *Contributors*: Dbenbenn, FML, Havang(nl), Mboverload

Image:AppleCapsLock.jpg *Source*: http://en.wikipedia.org/w/index.php?title=File:AppleCapsLock.jpg *License*: unknown *Contributors*: Original uploader was MartinRobinson at en.wikipedia

Image:KB United States-NoAltGr.svg *Source*: http://en.wikipedia.org/w/index.php?title=File:KB_United_States-NoAltGr.svg *License*: unknown *Contributors*: Deadcode, Edgar181, Edokter, Michaelliberty, NT27, SheeEttin, THEN WHO WAS PHONE?, 8 anonymous edits

Printed by Books on Demand GmbH, Norderstedt / Germany